ISBN: 9798303107595

Cover design by: Art Painter
Library of Congress Control Number: 2018675309
Printed in the United States of America

# FOREWORD

In the fall of 1991, I left the small-town familiarity of North Dallas, Texas, where I was raised after being born in Mexico, Missouri, for what would become a transformative journey across Europe. Over the next two decades, I lived, worked, and built a life across multiple countries, gaining firsthand experience of the promises and challenges of Europe's "free" healthcare and education systems.

Living in Switzerland, Italy, the United Kingdom, and France allowed me to see how these social welfare models functioned in practice—sometimes as idealized in policy, but often falling short in reality. My professional journey spanned industries and borders, exposing me to diverse healthcare frameworks, educational institutions, and social policies that shaped not only the societies around me but also my perspective on what it means when a government promises something "for free."

On a personal level, I married twice, both times to French women, and through these relationships, I gained even deeper insight into how European families navigate complex public systems. From securing quality healthcare to pursuing meaningful education for children, I encountered the reality behind the political slogans. I saw the triumphs and failures of public services from both a professional and family perspective, often experiencing the sharp contrast between what is promised and what is delivered.

This book is born from those years of living within Europe's public welfare systems—not as an outsider looking in but as someone embedded in the very fabric of its social structures. My goal is not to dismiss the ideals behind free healthcare and education, but to examine the often-overlooked costs, complexities, and compromises that come with them.

By sharing my experiences, observations, and research, I hope to illuminate the hidden trade-offs behind Europe's most celebrated social policies. This is not just an academic exploration; it is a deeply personal account shaped by years of living, working, and raising a family within the systems this book seeks to explore.

Welcome to *Promise or Peril: The Untold Truth About Free Healthcare and Education in Europe.* Let's uncover what lies beneath the surface of these widely celebrated promises—and what it truly costs to call something "free."

# CONTENTS

# INTRODUCTION

## Living Between Two Worlds

Having lived in Europe from 1992 to 2012 and returning to the United States in 2012, I have experienced both the promises and the pitfalls of government-driven welfare systems and free-market societies. My years in Europe exposed me to the realities of expansive state controled high taxes, overregulated markets, and welfare programs that often led to economic stagnation and personal dependency.

When I returned to the United States, I expected a landscape still driven by free enterprise and individual ambition. What I found instead was a country slowly drifting toward the same centralized policies I had left behind in Europe. Many young Americans seemed disillusioned, believing that government intervention could solve personal and societal challenges, ideas fueled by media narratives and political promises.

This book explores the stark differences I've lived through, between the social welfare state of Europe and the still-resilient but increasingly regulated U.S. economy. It examines how government policies impact personal freedom, economic opportunity, and cultural identity. Through comparative analysis and real-world stories, I break down how well-intentioned policies can undermine the very principles they claim to defend: equality, opportunity, and self-reliance.

I wrote this book to shine a light on the consequences of excessive state intervention while offering a path forward built on personal responsibility, limited government, and free-market innovation. I've lived the contrast, and now I invite you to explore the reality behind the rhetoric and decide which path offers the most freedom and opportunity for future generations.

**Chris l'Amerloc**

**Chapter 1**

# P UBLIC HEALTHCARE AND EDUCATION

*Background of public healthcare and education systems.*

Public healthcare and education have historically been regarded as equalizing forces, promising universal access and social mobility. However, decades of political interference, bureaucratic expansion, and economic mismanagement have transformed these systems into inefficient, state-controlled structures. This chapter examines how these essential services, originally designed to uplift society, have become entangled in political conflicts and economic stagnation.

It explores the historical development of public services, highlights their decline through mismanagement and political agendas, and proposes market-driven reforms emphasizing efficiency, accountability, and sustainable progress.

# Historical Vision Vs. Modern Reality

Public healthcare and education have long been regarded as fundamental pillars of modern civilization, envisioned as equalizing forces that guarantee essential services regardless of socioeconomic status. In theory, these systems aim to promote societal well-being, empower individuals through knowledge, and reduce economic disparities. However, the historical development of public healthcare and education reveals a more complex reality shaped by political, economic, and social agendas. Misconceptions about these services persist, influencing public discourse and policy-making.

# Historical Foundations

Early Healthcare and Education Systems

The earliest forms of public healthcare in Europe emerged from religious institutions during the medieval period, where hospitals provided charity care funded by churches and monarchs. Education followed a similar path, with religious orders controlling schools, ensuring that learning was limited to the elite.

pHowever, outside Europe, public welfare concepts also evolved. In ancient China, healthcare was guided by Confucian ideals emphasizing communal responsibility and mutual aid. Similarly, the Islamic world advanced medical science during the medieval era through state-supported hospitals like the renowned Al-Qarawiyyin in Morocco and the Bimaristan in Baghdad, fostering innovations that influenced Western medicine.

## State Involvement Begins

The Industrial Revolution of the 18th and 19th centuries forced European and American governments to intervene in public health and education. Industrial urban centers faced severe outbreaks of diseases like cholera and typhoid, prompting state-led sanitation campaigns. In Britain, the Public Health Act of 1848 established local health boards, while in the U.S., cities like New York launched sanitation reforms that laid the groundwork for modern public health systems.

Education reforms paralleled these efforts. The rise of industrial economies required a literate, skilled workforce, pushing governments to enact compulsory schooling laws. In Prussia, the state pioneered universal education, inspiring similar reforms across Europe and North America. In the U.S., Horace Mann's advocacy led to public schooling systems focused on civic responsibility and industrial productivity.

# Expanding Access In The 20Th Century

The socio-economic upheavals following two world wars accelerated welfare-state expansions in Europe and the Americas. In 1948, Britain established the National Health Service (NHS), guaranteeing healthcare as a universal right. In the U.S., Medicare and Medicaid were introduced in the 1960s, providing healthcare access to seniors and low-income citizens.

Public education also saw transformative reforms. Following World War II, the U.S. enacted the GI Bill, expanding college access to millions of returning veterans. In Europe, free secondary education became standard, fostering an educated post-war generation that drove economic recovery and social mobility.

# The Promise Of Equality Vs. Political Agendas

Despite being framed as tools of equality, both public healthcare and education have often been shaped by political motives. Welfare systems frequently became vehicles for social control, as political leaders sought to reduce civil unrest by offering free services while preserving power structures.

### Healthcare as a Political Tool

Throughout history, healthcare reforms have often been linked to political campaigns promising "free" medical care in exchange for voter support. Government-funded healthcare programs are prone to political interference, resulting in waste, corruption, and mismanagement.

Political agendas frequently divert funds from public services to politically favorable projects. In South Africa, education reforms aimed at promoting equality have been undermined by corruption, with millions lost to misallocated funds.

### Education as Social Engineering

Public education systems have also been used for political and cultural indoctrination. Curriculums have been adjusted throughout history to promote state-approved ideologies, from nationalist agendas in early 20th-century Europe to modern identity-based education in today's classrooms.

Progressive policies have turned public education into a battleground for ideological control, with Critical Race Theory (CRT) and identity politics replacing traditional academic excellence. Government-mandated healthcare programs, such as the Affordable Care Act (ACA), have reduced patient choice and driven up premiums by enforcing one-size-fits-all policies

# Modern-Day Challenges

Today, public healthcare and education systems face unprecedented challenges rooted in their historical structures, expanded bureaucracies, and shifting political narratives.

### Healthcare Systems in Crisis

Public healthcare struggles with increasing costs, long wait times, and limited access to specialized care. Government-managed health services in countries like the UK and Canada frequently face budget cuts, staff shortages, and overburdened hospitals. In the U.S., attempts to socialize healthcare through the Affordable Care Act (ACA) introduced government mandates that disrupted private insurance markets while failing to reduce costs for most Americans.

### Educational Decline

Public education has become a battleground for cultural and ideological conflicts. Standardized testing, outdated teaching methods, and a lack of school choice have led to declining educational outcomes. Meanwhile, rising student debt in the U.S. has turned higher education into a financial burden rather than a pathway to upward mobility.

*Examples of How Left-Leaning Policies Have Challenged Healthcare and Education Systems*

# Healthcare Systems In Crisis

## Affordable Care Act (Aca) - U.s. Example:

**What Happened:** The ACA, passed under the Obama Administration in 2010, aimed to provide universal healthcare by expanding Medicaid and mandating insurance coverage. However, it created complex regulations and required individuals to buy health insurance or face penalties.

**Impact:**

**Private Market Disruption:** Millions lost existing health plans because they did not meet government-mandated standards. The promise of "if you like your doctor, you can keep your doctor" proved false.

**Skyrocketing Premiums:** Insurance premiums rose, particularly for middle-class Americans, as insurers passed the costs of expanded coverage onto consumers.

**Provider Shortages:** An increased patient load on public and private systems overwhelmed already-strained healthcare providers, resulting in longer wait times and service rationing.

# Nhs Budget Cuts - Uk Example

As of 2023, the average wait time for elective surgeries under the UK's NHS is over 12 months, according to NHS Digital. In the U.S., student loan debt has surpassed $1.7 trillion, with the average borrower owing $37,000. These figures highlight the growing burden on public systems globally.

**What Happened:** Despite being a cornerstone of the UK's welfare system, the National Health Service (NHS) has faced persistent underfunding and bureaucratic mismanagement due to politically driven budget cuts.

**Impact:**

**Service Delays:** Patients routinely wait months for surgeries, specialist appointments, and even cancer treatments.

**Overburdened Hospitals:** Many hospitals operate beyond capacity, forcing patients to wait in emergency rooms for basic care.

**Political Scandals:** The NHS has been plagued by procurement scandals and wasteful spending, often exposed during government transitions.

# Canada's Single-Payer Healthcare Struggles:

**What Happened:** Canada's government-run healthcare system promises free care but suffers from chronic underfunding and staff shortages.

**Impact:**

**Medical Tourism:** Wealthier Canadians travel abroad for faster treatment.

**Critical Care Delays:** Diagnostic services like MRIs and surgeries often face six-month to one-year wait times, risking patients' lives.

# Educational Decline

# Common Core Standards - U.s. Example:

**What Happened:** Introduced in 2009 under the Obama Administration, Common Core aimed to standardize educational benchmarks across states but faced widespread criticism for bureaucratic overreach and ineffective implementation.

**Impact:**

**One-Size-Fits-All Curriculum:** Teachers were forced to follow rigid guidelines that prioritized standardized testing over real learning.

**Declining Performance:** Test scores in math and reading have stagnated or dropped since Common Core's adoption, especially in underfunded school districts.

**Teacher Burnout:** Educators faced overwhelming administrative burdens and reduced classroom autonomy.

# France's Centralized Education System:

**What Happened:** France's government-run education system heavily regulates school curricula, leaving little room for innovation or local input.

**Impact:**

**Academic Decline:** French schools have seen declining student performance in international rankings for math and science.

**Political Indoctrination:** Critics argue that the system promotes secularism and leftist ideology while downplaying historical and cultural heritage.

## Germany's Dual-System Limitations:

**What Happened:** While Germany's education system is often praised, its rigid tracking system funnels students into vocational or academic paths at a young age, often based on early test scores.

**Impact:**

**Social Inequality:** Lower-income and immigrant families face systemic disadvantages, limiting social mobility.

**Limited Flexibility:** Students stuck in vocational tracks face difficulty transitioning to higher education, reinforcing class divides.

## Student Loan Debt Crisis - U.s. Example:

**What Happened:** U.S. universities saw tuition skyrocket due to unlimited access to federally guaranteed student loans under policies expanded by the Obama Administration.

**Impact:**

**Rising Tuition Costs:** Colleges increased tuition unchecked, knowing that students could borrow more from the government.

**Crippling Debt:** Student debt surpassed $1.7 trillion, burdening young professionals with decades of loan repayment.

**Lower Return on Investment:** College degrees no longer guarantee good-paying jobs, contributing to disillusionment with the higher education system.

## Underlying Cause - Left-Leaning Policy Failures

**Centralized Control:** Socialized models increase government control, reducing individual choice and creating massive bureaucratic systems prone to inefficiency.

**Political Agendas:** Education and healthcare systems become battlegrounds for political narratives, diverting attention from real reforms.

**Unsustainable Funding Models:** High taxes and mismanaged budgets drain resources while failing to deliver promised services.

## Economic Consequences

### Funding Gaps and Inefficiency

Both public healthcare and education systems suffer from chronic underfunding and mismanagement, driven by wasteful spending and politically motivated budget allocations. Mismanagement often stems from excessive administrative costs, where a disproportionate share of budgets is allocated to non-essential bureaucratic roles rather than frontline services. For example, in the U.S. education system, administrative expenditures have outpaced spending on teacher salaries, leading to crowded classrooms and teacher shortages despite increased educational funding.

Politically motivated funding cuts also exacerbate the issue. Lawmakers may redirect funds toward high-visibility projects that garner voter support, leaving critical but less politically advantageous programs underfunded. In healthcare, shifting federal budget priorities have led to reduced allocations for preventive care programs, causing long-term healthcare costs to balloon due to avoidable chronic diseases.

**Overregulation and Bureaucratic Bloat**

Government-run services are inherently bureaucratic, creating slow, inefficient systems that resist reform. Complex administrative structures often consume a significant portion of allocated funds, diverting resources from essential services such as patient care in hospitals or student support in schools. Overregulation further compounds the issue by requiring compliance with cumbersome legal frameworks that stifle innovation and inflate operational costs.

## Case Study: The U.s. Department Of Veterans Affairs (Va)

The VA serves as a stark example of bureaucratic bloat and administrative inefficiency. The department has faced numerous scandals related to mismanagement and delayed services. A 2014 audit revealed that some veterans waited months for medical appointments due to systemic scheduling failures, despite significant budget increases over the years. Much of the problem was attributed to excessive layers of management, redundant oversight committees, and outdated IT systems that complicated service delivery. This bureaucratic sprawl has led to billions in wasted taxpayer dollars while many veterans continue to struggle to access timely care.

## Present-Day Reality - Social And Political Manipulation

Public healthcare and education have become deeply intertwined with political narratives, making genuine reform difficult. In many countries, these systems are now tools for expanding government control, ensuring voter loyalty, and advancing ideological agendas.

# Healthcare As A Right Or Privilege?

The debate over whether healthcare is a human right or a service has fueled intense political battles. Advocates of universal healthcare argue that access to medical care is a fundamental human right that governments must guarantee. In contrast, opponents warn that government-managed systems risk inefficiency, long wait times, and rationed care, leaving the wealthy as the only group able to afford timely private services.

**Contrasting Views:**

- **Political Leaders:** U.S. Senator Bernie Sanders has consistently advocated for "Medicare for All," emphasizing healthcare as a right. Meanwhile, opponents like Senator Mitch McConnell argue that such policies would create unsustainable costs and erode personal choice.
- **Healthcare Advocacy Organizations:** Groups like Physicians for a National Health Program champion single-payer healthcare systems, while the Heritage Foundation highlights concerns over reduced care quality and innovation under government-run models.

# Education As Cultural Warfare

In modern classrooms, traditional academic subjects increasingly compete with politically driven curriculums focused on social issues, identity politics, and cultural activism. The result is an education system that often prioritizes ideological conformity over critical thinking and real-world skills.

*In France, state-driven curricula have faced backlash for promoting secularism while downplaying cultural heritage education. In*

*Brazil, politically influenced curriculum reforms have been criticized for omitting indigenous history and minimizing the country's dictatorship-era abuses.*

**Key Legislative Efforts & Court Cases:**

- **Critical Race Theory (CRT) Debates:** State legislatures across the U.S. have passed laws restricting the teaching of CRT, arguing that it promotes division. Supporters maintain that CRT helps address systemic racism and historical inequities.
- **School Choice Battles:** The U.S. Supreme Court case *Espinoza v. Montana Department of Revenue* (2020) upheld the use of public funding for religious schools, fueling ongoing debates over school vouchers and public education funding.
- **Curriculum Restrictions:** States like Florida and Texas have introduced laws limiting how race, gender identity, and American history are taught, reflecting broader cultural battles over what constitutes a "neutral" curriculum.

These conflicts illustrate how public education has become a battleground for ideological influence, often leaving students caught between competing narratives rather than receiving a well-rounded, unbiased education.

# Unfulfilled Promises, Urgent Reforms

Despite decades of promises from policymakers, public healthcare and education systems continue to fall short of their potential. Rising costs, bureaucratic inefficiencies, and political entanglements have left millions underserved. The gap between promises and reality demands urgent reforms to ensure accessible, efficient, and high-quality services for all.

# Actionable Recommendations:

1. **Public-Private Partnerships:**

- Encourage collaborations between governments and private sector organizations to leverage innovation, reduce costs, and increase efficiency. In healthcare, this could involve outsourcing non-essential services or establishing hybrid care models. In education, industry partnerships could modernize vocational training and STEM programs.

2.        **School Choice Policies:**

- Implement school choice initiatives such as charter schools, vouchers, and education savings accounts (ESAs) to empower parents with more control over their children's education. Competition among schools can drive improvements in quality and innovation.

3.        **Healthcare Deregulation:**

- Simplify healthcare regulations to reduce administrative burdens, increase competition, and lower costs. Deregulating insurance markets, streamlining medical licensing, and expanding telehealth services can enhance care accessibility.

4.        **Performance-Based Funding:**

- Tie government funding to measurable outcomes in both sectors. Schools could be evaluated based on student performance, while hospitals could be rated on patient outcomes, wait times, and operational efficiency.

5.        **Decentralization of Services:**

- Shift decision-making power from centralized bureaucracies to local authorities, schools, and healthcare providers. This would enable tailored solutions that reflect the specific needs of communities.

The future of public healthcare and education hangs in the balance. Without decisive action, economic stagnation, declining global competitiveness, and widening social divides are inevitable. Policymakers must rise above partisan agendas and commit to transformative reforms that prioritize efficiency, accountability, and individual choice. Inaction is not just a policy failure—it's a betrayal of future generations. The time to act is now.

Public services should serve the people, not political agendas. By embracing market-driven reforms, holding policymakers accountable, and fostering innovation, we can build a future where healthcare and education truly provide equal opportunity for all.

# Origins Of Public Healthcare

The roots of public healthcare trace back to ancient civilizations, where collective responsibility for health emerged from practical necessity. Societies like Egypt, Greece, and Rome prioritized sanitation, clean water systems, and disease prevention as public health concerns. They built aqueducts, bathhouses, and early hospitals to serve both military and civilian populations. Public health efforts were tied to religion, politics, and social stability, with temples in Greece offering medical care through priests of Asclepius, the god of healing.

## Healthcare in Medieval Europe

During the Middle Ages, Europe faced epidemics like the Black Death, prompting communities to establish hospitals managed by religious institutions such as monasteries and churches. These early hospitals focused on care rather than cure, offering shelter, nourishment, and basic medical attention to the sick and poor.

## Example: Hôtel-Dieu in France

France played a significant role in the early development of public healthcare. The *Hôtel-Dieu de Paris*, founded in the 7th century, remains one of the oldest hospitals in the world. Initially a religious charity, it provided free care to the poor, reflecting the era's belief in healthcare as a Christian duty rather than a state function.

**Common Misconception:**

*Public healthcare is a modern, socialist concept.*

**Reality:**

Public healthcare's origins are ancient and deeply rooted in notions of communal care and social responsibility. In medieval Europe, healthcare was not state-run but community-driven through religious institutions and charitable donations.

**The Enlightenment and State Involvement**

The Enlightenment reshaped healthcare with ideas of rationalism, human rights, and scientific progress. Governments began recognizing healthcare as essential for public stability. France's experience during the French Revolution marked a shift toward state responsibility. The revolutionaries aimed to create a more equitable society, leading to early state-funded health initiatives like military hospitals and vaccination campaigns.

**France's Influence on Modern Healthcare**

France's long-standing tradition of combining public and private healthcare laid the groundwork for its modern system. The French Revolution institutionalized social welfare through laws like the 1794 decree requiring hospitals to care for all citizens. Napoleon's administration expanded military healthcare infrastructure, influencing public health models worldwide.

**Global Impact**

While Britain's Public Health Act of 1848 is often cited as a major milestone, France's contributions predate it and emphasize the gradual evolution of public healthcare from religious charity to state-supported institutions. This development was driven by the need to address pandemics, improve living conditions, and maintain societal stability.

# Rise Of Modern Healthcare Systems

The Industrial Revolution dramatically reshaped societies, transforming rural communities into densely populated cities. This rapid urbanization led to overcrowded living conditions, poor sanitation, and the unchecked spread of infectious diseases like cholera, tuberculosis, and influenza. The public healthcare systems we recognize today emerged as a response to these crises, evolving from rudimentary care into organized, state-funded institutions.

**Key Milestones in Modern Public Healthcare**

## Bismarck Model (Germany, 1883)

**What Happened?**
Germany introduced the world's first national healthcare system under Chancellor Otto von Bismarck. Employers and employees were required to contribute to sickness funds, ensuring access to medical care and wage compensation during illness.

**Positive Impacts:**

- Set the precedent for modern social insurance models.
- Reduced preventable mortality rates.
- Strengthened the relationship between labor rights and healthcare access.

**Negative Impacts:**

- Limited initially to industrial workers, excluding large portions of the population.
- Relied on a complex administrative structure that increased government oversight of private healthcare providers.

# Beveridge Model (Uk, 1948)

### What Happened?

Post-World War II Britain created the National Health Service (NHS), offering healthcare free at the point of use. Funded through general taxation, the NHS provided universal coverage regardless of income.

### Positive Impacts:

- Healthcare became a right, not a privilege.
- Reduced health inequality by removing financial barriers.
- Inspired similar models worldwide, especially in Europe and Commonwealth countries.

### Negative Impacts:

- Expensive to maintain, requiring continuous tax adjustments.
- Long wait times and resource shortages due to increased demand.
- Bureaucratic complexity with evolving public expectations.

# Medicare And Medicaid (Usa, 1965)

### What Happened?

U.S. President Lyndon B. Johnson signed legislation creating Medicare (for seniors) and Medicaid (for low-income individuals). These programs represented a significant expansion of federal involvement in healthcare.

### Positive Impacts:

- Expanded access to healthcare for millions of elderly and vulnerable individuals.
- Reduced poverty among older Americans through health cost coverage.

### Negative Impacts:

- High administrative costs due to the complexity of U.S. healthcare.
- Persistent gaps in coverage, particularly for the uninsured.
- Controversies over privatization and rising healthcare expenditures.

## France's Contribution: A Hybrid Model

While Germany and Britain laid the foundations for public healthcare, France pursued a hybrid approach blending public and private services. In 1945, France established a system of *Sécurité Sociale*, funded by payroll taxes and overseen by the state.

### Positive Impacts

- Ensured comprehensive coverage for the majority of its citizens.
- Allowed choice between public and private healthcare providers.
- Became one of the most highly regarded healthcare systems globally.

### Negative Impacts

- High tax burdens to sustain the system.
- Complicated administrative processes.
- Periodic strikes by healthcare workers demanding better pay and conditions.

## Broader Impacts: Good And Bad

### Good Impacts

### Global Health Improvements:

- Vaccination campaigns eradicated diseases like smallpox.
- Public hospitals and clinics increased life expectancy.

### Social Equity

- Healthcare access became less dependent on wealth or social class in many countries.
- Reduced the social stigma of seeking medical care.

## Economic Productivity

- Healthier workforces boosted national productivity and reduced economic losses from epidemics.

## Negative Impacts

## Rising Costs

- Public healthcare systems require substantial funding through taxation, creating a financial burden in times of economic downturn.

## Bureaucratic Inefficiency

- Centralized healthcare systems often face administrative delays and complex regulatory frameworks.

## Political Weaponization

- Healthcare reforms can be politically charged, leading to policy instability during government transitions.

## Access Disparities

- Even in well-funded systems, rural and marginalized communities often experience limited healthcare access.

# The Rise Of Modern Healthcare Systems

The journey from rudimentary public health practices to state-funded healthcare systems reflects humanity's enduring struggle to balance compassion with practicality. The Industrial Revolution exposed the harsh realities of rapid urbanization, forcing societies to confront the need for organized healthcare on a national scale. In response, models like Germany's Bismarck System and Britain's National Health Service emerged, setting historical precedents that continue to shape healthcare policies around the world.

While public healthcare systems have achieved remarkable successes—such as eradicating deadly diseases, improving life expectancy, and promoting social equity—they have also faced persistent challenges. Bureaucratic inefficiencies, rising costs, and politically driven reforms have plagued even the most developed systems. Access disparities remain a stubborn issue, with marginalized communities frequently left behind despite expanded coverage.

France's hybrid system stands as an example of how blending public and private healthcare can yield impressive results but at the cost of high taxation and complex administration. Similarly, the U.S. experiment with Medicare and Medicaid highlights both the potential and limitations of government intervention in a predominantly privatized system.

The rise of modern healthcare reveals a fundamental tension between idealism and reality: the desire to ensure equitable healthcare for all versus the economic and logistical challenges of delivering it. As healthcare systems continue to evolve, the key to sustainability lies in striking a balance—embracing innovation, reducing waste, ensuring accountability, and fostering cooperation between the public and private sectors. Only by learning from past successes and failures can societies craft healthcare systems that are both compassionate and resilient, ensuring that the promise of modern medicine becomes a lasting reality for future generations.

## Public Education's Early Foundations

Education has long been a fundamental institution shaping societies. Its origins were deeply rooted in religious instruction and moral guidance, gradually evolving into state-sponsored models aimed at creating literate, law-abiding citizens. While public education is often viewed as a tool for enlightenment, its historical development reveals its role in advancing political, social, and economic agendas.

## Ancient Beginnings: Education As Civic Duty

The earliest formal education systems emerged in ancient civilizations like Sumer, Egypt, and China, where literacy was essential for administrative roles in temple and state bureaucracies. Education was initially reserved for elites—scribes, priests, and aristocrats—tasked with managing state affairs and religious ceremonies.

**Ancient Greece:**
Education flourished in ancient Greece, where city-states like Athens and Sparta implemented distinct educational models reflecting their societal goals.

- **Athens:** Education focused on cultivating civic responsibility, critical thinking, and rhetoric. Philosophers like Socrates, Plato, and Aristotle laid the foundations for liberal arts education.
- **Sparta:** Education was militaristic, emphasizing physical training, discipline, and loyalty to the state.

Both systems linked education directly to state needs—whether for governance or warfare—foreshadowing future models of state-controlled education.

## Religious Foundations In The Middle Ages

The fall of the Roman Empire shifted educational responsibility to the Christian Church in Europe. Monasteries, cathedrals, and abbeys became centers of learning, preserving ancient texts and teaching religious doctrine.

- **Monastic Schools:** Focused on religious studies, reading, writing, and Latin.

- **Cathedral Schools:** Educated clergy and future leaders, evolving into early universities.

**The Rise of Universities:**
The 11th and 12th centuries saw the emergence of Europe's first universities, including the University of Bologna (1088), the University of Paris (1150), and the University of Oxford (1167). These institutions blended religious study with secular subjects like law, medicine, and philosophy, establishing the intellectual foundations for modern education systems.

**Common Misconception:**
*Public education was designed solely to enlighten the masses.*

**Reality:**
While public education undoubtedly advanced literacy and intellectual development, its broader purpose extended far beyond enlightenment. Throughout history, it served political, social, and economic functions, including:

**1. Political Agendas:**

- **Nation-Building:** Education promoted national identity through state-approved curricula, emphasizing shared languages, histories, and cultural values.
- **Social Control:** Governments used education to instill loyalty, obedience, and conformity. This was particularly evident in authoritarian regimes where indoctrination was central.

**2. Economic Needs:**

- **Industrial Revolution:** With the rise of industrial economies, education became a means to produce disciplined, skilled workers.
- **Technical Training:** Many countries developed vocational schools to meet the demands of growing industries.

**3. Social Hierarchies:**

- **Social Stratification:** While public education aimed to equalize opportunities, it often reinforced class divisions through selective access to advanced education and prestigious institutions.

- **Gender Inequality:** For centuries, education was primarily reserved for men, while women were educated in domestic skills or excluded altogether.

## Education Reforms In Early Modern Europe

The Enlightenment and Age of Reason (17th-18th centuries) catalyzed major educational reforms, emphasizing reason, science, and human rights. Thinkers like John Locke, Jean-Jacques Rousseau, and Immanuel Kant argued for education as a public good essential for an enlightened and just society.

- **France's Influence:** Revolutionary France's secular education reforms laid the groundwork for modern public schooling. The 1791 Constitution declared education a public right, while the Napoleonic Code reorganized schools to serve both civic and military needs.
- **Prussia's Model:** Prussia developed one of the earliest state-controlled education systems in the 18th century, combining military discipline with literacy training, influencing systems in Europe and the United States.

## Global Expansion Of Public Education

By the 19th century, industrializing nations recognized that educating the masses was essential for economic development and social stability. Compulsory education laws spread across Europe, the United States, and Japan, ensuring that children attended school and learned standardized curricula focused on reading, writing, arithmetic, and moral values.

**Key Developments:**

- **United States:** Horace Mann championed universal public education in the mid-1800s, shaping the American public school system.

- **France:** The 1881-1882 Jules Ferry Laws mandated free, secular, and compulsory education, emphasizing civic responsibility.
- **Japan:** Following the Meiji Restoration, Japan rapidly modernized its education system to strengthen national power.

## Broader Impacts Of Early Public Education

**Positive Impacts:**

- **Increased Literacy:** Expanding access to education drastically improved literacy rates worldwide.
- **Social Mobility:** Education became a pathway to economic and social advancement.
- **Cultural Preservation:** Schools preserved and transmitted cultural heritage and national histories.

**Negative Impacts:**

- **Cultural Erasure:** Colonial powers used education to impose their languages, religions, and values on colonized peoples.
- **Social Inequality:** Educational systems often reinforced existing social hierarchies by limiting access for marginalized communities.
- **Political Indoctrination:** Authoritarian states manipulated education to maintain power and suppress dissent.

## The Transformation Of Public Education - Power, Politics, And Progress

Public education has evolved from religious instruction and elite training into one of society's most essential institutions, shaping nations, economies, and cultures. Its journey from ancient civilizations to modern state-sponsored systems reflects humanity's ongoing struggle to balance knowledge dissemination with political, social, and economic control.

The earliest education systems were tools for maintaining religious and political power, reserved for elites tasked with governing and preserving cultural legacies. Ancient Greek models, the rise of monastic and cathedral schools, and the creation of medieval universities laid the intellectual foundations that still influence educational institutions today. With the Industrial Revolution and the rise of nation-states, education shifted from privilege to necessity, producing literate, disciplined workers essential for economic growth and military power.

However, the expansion of public education has been far from universally benevolent. While it has undoubtedly increased literacy, advanced scientific progress, and fostered social mobility, it has also been weaponized as a tool of political indoctrination, cultural assimilation, and social stratification. Throughout history, governments have used education to strengthen national identities, control populations, and reinforce societal hierarchies.

The dual legacy of public education remains relevant today. While modern schooling is more accessible and inclusive than ever before, it continues to grapple with historical inequalities, cultural tensions, and shifting ideological influences. Political agendas still shape curricula, while educational inequities persist, often leaving marginalized communities behind.

The lesson from this historical journey is clear: education must be more than a political instrument or economic necessity. It should cultivate independent thinking, foster innovation, and empower individuals to build better societies. For public education to truly fulfill its promise, it must resist the pull of state control and ideological manipulation, remaining committed to its core mission of enlightenment, opportunity, and intellectual freedom.

# Expansion Of Modern Education Systems From Industrial Needs To Political Agendas

The expansion of modern education systems in the 19th and 20th centuries was driven primarily by industrial, economic, and political forces, rather than a pure desire to enlighten the masses. As governments recognized the need for a literate, disciplined workforce, education evolved into a state-controlled mechanism designed to meet the demands of rapidly industrializing economies and expanding empires. While reforms increased access to education, they also entrenched government control, standardization, and ideological indoctrination, shaping modern societies in profound and often problematic ways.

## Key Developments In Modern Education

## 1. Compulsory Education Laws: Creating A Compliant Workforce

Governments worldwide passed compulsory education laws, mandating school attendance to combat child labor while producing a trained labor force for industrial economies. These policies were less about intellectual empowerment and more about creating a workforce tailored to meet the needs of expanding industries.

The Industrial Revolution demanded workers who could read instructions, perform basic calculations, and follow orders in factories, mines, and assembly lines. Compulsory schooling provided a steady pipeline of factory-ready laborers while removing children from the labor force, ensuring that adults could occupy those jobs.

**Real Impact:**

- **Improved Literacy Rates:** Public education systems did raise global literacy levels and allowed more people to participate in the emerging industrial economy.
- **Standardized Learning:** Schools emphasized discipline, punctuality, and repetitive learning—traits essential to the efficiency-driven industrial model.
- **Social Conditioning:** Classrooms mirrored factory environments, reinforcing authority, obedience, and routine tasks over critical thinking or intellectual exploration.

## 2. The Progressive Education Movement (Usa, Early 20Th Century)

Emerging in the United States, the Progressive Education Movement challenged rigid, authoritarian schooling systems by promoting hands-on, student-centered learning. Advocates like **John Dewey** believed that education should prepare students for participation in a democratic society, emphasizing personal growth, critical thinking, and social responsibility.

Industrialization and rapid urbanization led to social instability, poverty, and inequality. Reformers sought to humanize education, making it more inclusive and relevant to real-world experiences. They argued that teaching should go beyond rote memorization to prepare individuals for civic engagement.

**Real Impact:**

- **Limited Systemic Change:** While some schools adopted progressive methods, most public systems remained focused on conformity, obedience, and job training.
- **Experiments vs. Reality:** Experimental schools flourished in wealthy areas, but mainstream public education

was constrained by bureaucratic policies, overcrowded classrooms, and rigid state curricula.

- **Political Redirection:** Progressive ideals were often diluted or politically co-opted to serve state agendas, reinforcing conformity under the guise of democratic education.

# 3. Post-War Educational Reforms: Nation-Building Through Learning

Following both World Wars, nations expanded access to secondary and higher education to rebuild war-torn economies and secure geopolitical dominance. Education became a national priority as technological advancement, military preparedness, and economic competitiveness became essential to global influence.

- **Reconstruction Efforts:** Post-war economies needed skilled engineers, scientists, and technologists to drive innovation and rebuild infrastructure.
- **Cold War Competition:** The ideological battle between the U.S. and the Soviet Union during the Cold War intensified investments in STEM education to ensure military superiority and space exploration success.
- **Social Stability:** Expanding education provided a pathway to social mobility, reducing social unrest and reinforcing national unity.

**Real Impact:**

- **Technological Advancements:** Universities transformed into state-sponsored research hubs focused on military and industrial innovation, often at the expense of the arts and humanities.
- **Global Power Structures:** Countries like the U.S., the USSR, and Western Europe used education to assert geopolitical

dominance through scientific achievements and ideological outreach.

- **Social Stratification:** While education expanded, access to prestigious institutions remained highly selective, preserving elite control and perpetuating social inequalities.

## The Hidden Costs Of Expansion

While the expansion of modern education systems led to undeniable progress in literacy, technological development, and social mobility, it also entrenched state control, bureaucratic inefficiency, and cultural conformity. What was framed as a public good frequently served as a political tool, ensuring that students became productive workers, loyal citizens, and cultural adherents of state-approved ideologies.

Governments structured schools not only to educate but also to maintain political stability and economic productivity. Critical thinking, creativity, and intellectual independence were often sacrificed for efficiency, obedience, and economic expediency. The legacy of these developments continues to shape modern education systems, making meaningful reform a persistent challenge.

Would you like further elaboration on any of these sections or additional historical examples?

## Persistent Realities And Challenges

Public healthcare and education systems, while foundational to modern society, are plagued by systemic flaws rooted in government mismanagement, political corruption, and special-interest influence. Far from being efficient or altruistic, these systems frequently serve political agendas rather than public welfare, leaving taxpayers burdened by subpar services and entrenched bureaucratic structures resistant to meaningful reform.

## Reality 1: Public Services Are Inefficient Compared To Private Ones

Public healthcare and education are often characterized by inefficiency, mismanagement, and bureaucratic red tape. Governments routinely misallocate funds, inflate budgets, and prioritize political interests over public welfare. Private providers, driven by competition and profit, are inherently more efficient, innovative, and results-oriented because their survival depends on delivering superior customer satisfaction.

**The Truth:**

1.    **Bureaucratic Inefficiency:**
Public services operate within sprawling administrative systems filled with redundant procedures, overlapping agencies, and political interference. Layers of decision-making create delays, miscommunication, and missed opportunities for meaningful reform. In contrast, private institutions adapt quickly and respond directly to market demands.

2.    **Corruption and Mismanagement:**
Government contracts are often awarded through nepotism, lobbying, and political favoritism. In healthcare, pharmaceutical companies influence public health policies to promote long-term medication use rather than pursue cures. In education, ideological interests shape curricula, promoting politically driven narratives over objective knowledge.

3.      **Lack of Innovation:**

Public institutions are slow to innovate due to rigid government policies, budget limitations, and union-backed job protections. By contrast, private companies continuously innovate to remain profitable and attract clients. Examples include:

- **Private Healthcare:** Advanced diagnostics, cutting-edge treatments, and personalized care.
- **Private Education:** Modern teaching methods, individualized learning plans, and technology-driven instruction.

4.      **Political Influence and Indoctrination:**

Public education frequently reflects government-sanctioned narratives, shaping young minds according to state-approved ideologies. Critical thinking is often replaced by standardized testing designed to produce compliant, state-serving citizens rather than independent thinkers.

5.      **Lack of Accountability:**

Public institutions rarely face consequences for underperformance. Private providers must meet high expectations or risk closure, ensuring a constant push for excellence. By contrast, public services—protected by unions and taxpayer funding—often shield mediocrity from market pressures.

# Reality 2: Public Healthcare Means Longer Wait Times And Lower Quality Care

**Why the Perception Exists:**

Reports of long wait times, rationed care, and overwhelmed public hospitals have fueled negative perceptions of public healthcare, particularly in countries like Canada and the UK.

**The Truth:**

1.         **Profit vs. Dependency:**
Private hospitals provide fast, efficient service because patient satisfaction directly affects their revenue. In public healthcare systems funded by taxes, demand often exceeds supply, causing delays, rationing, and reduced care quality.

2.         **Special Interests:**
Public healthcare systems are frequently influenced by pharmaceutical companies lobbying for long-term treatment plans rather than one-time cures, ensuring continuous revenue from chronic conditions. This incentivizes dependency rather than preventive care or groundbreaking medical advancements.

3.         **Lower Standards:**
Staff in public hospitals often face limited performance-based evaluations due to union protections and government job security. Private providers, competing for clients, invest in training, modern facilities, and exceptional staff to maintain their reputations and market share.

## Reality 3: Public Education Stifles Innovation And Creativity

**Why the Perception Exists:**

Public schools are often portrayed as stagnant institutions focused on rote memorization and standardized testing. Teachers have limited freedom to adapt curricula due to government mandates, leading to suppressed creativity and diminished learning outcomes.

**The Truth:**

1.	**Curriculum Control:**
Public education is designed to produce compliant, state-serving individuals through a standardized curriculum. Critical subjects like entrepreneurship, financial literacy, and independent thinking are often neglected or replaced by politically motivated narratives.

2.	**Union Protections:**
Unions frequently block meaningful educational reforms, ensuring that underperforming teachers remain employed while reducing incentives for high-achieving educators. Private schools, by contrast, hire and retain staff based on merit and performance.

3.	**Political Agendas:**
Public education has become a tool for ideological indoctrination, emphasizing specific worldviews while neglecting practical life skills. Private schools, with greater curricular independence, often focus on STEM, business, and the arts, fostering both intellectual growth and creative development.

# Reality 4: Public Services Are Not Free

**Why the Misconception Exists:**

The term "public" is often equated with "free," leading many to believe that public healthcare and education come at no cost, ignoring the significant tax burden required to fund these services.

**The Truth:**

1.	**Funded by Taxes:**
Public services are financed through income, sales, and property taxes. The more extensive the public welfare system, the higher the tax burden. Countries like Sweden

and Denmark offer comprehensive services but impose some of the world's highest tax rates.

2.      **Hidden Costs:**

Even in universal healthcare systems, costs such as prescription fees, supplemental insurance, and private tutoring remain common. Free public education often comes with out-of-pocket expenses for supplies, extracurriculars, and specialized programs.

3.      **Economic Trade-Off:**

Tax-funded services discourage personal responsibility. Many citizens opt for private alternatives, paying twice—once through taxes and again out-of-pocket for higher-quality service.

# Challenges And Policy Complexities

1.                      **Funding Shortfalls:** Governments frequently mismanage budgets, diverting funds from essential services to political pet projects. This results in underfunded schools, hospitals, and infrastructure.

2.                      **Political Instability:** Election cycles drive short-term policies that neglect long-term reforms. Public services suffer from inconsistent leadership and shifting priorities.

3.                      **Access Disparities:** Rural and marginalized communities are often left behind, facing staffing shortages, crumbling facilities, and minimal government investment.

4.                      **Resource Misallocation:** Governments frequently focus on symptomatic fixes rather than root causes, enriching contractors while ignoring sustainable, long-term solutions.

## The Path Forward

The only viable path forward lies in reducing government overreach, increasing transparency, and embracing free-market reforms. Expanding school choice, deregulating healthcare markets, and holding officials accountable would restore personal freedom and empower consumers.

Public services must be **accountable**, **efficient**, and **focused on real results**—not politically driven projects. Without meaningful reform, public services will continue serving political elites rather than the average citizen. **Personal responsibility, competition, and decentralization** are the only lasting solutions to reclaiming the original promise of public healthcare and education.

Chapter 2

# ECONOMIC REALITIES

## Funding Models and Hidden Costs

Public healthcare and education systems are frequently portrayed as free or low-cost services funded by taxpayers, promising universal access and equal opportunities. However, the economic realities reveal hidden costs, inefficient funding models, and unintended societal consequences. Instead of fostering prosperity, these systems often create dependency, suppress individual ambition, and reduce productivity. Drawing from personal experiences in Europe, this chapter explores how well-intentioned welfare policies can entrap citizens in cycles of reliance and economic stagnation, while proposing reforms that balance social safety nets with personal responsibility.

# The Welfare Trap

## Social Benefits vs. Economic Productivity

Government-provided social benefits are designed to support individuals in times of need, but in many European countries, these benefits have become long-term entitlements that discourage work and self-sufficiency. The ease of accessing welfare benefits leads many individuals to manipulate the system, ensuring they receive maximum financial aid while contributing minimally to the economy.

Key Patterns Observed:

**1. Preference for Cash Jobs:**

- Many individuals on welfare prefer cash-based jobs to avoid declaring income, ensuring they continue receiving full social benefits such as housing stipends, free healthcare, and child allowances.
- The underground economy thrives, with entire sectors operating outside legal tax frameworks, further burdening the state's finances.

**2. The "Social Benefit Lifestyle":**

- Long-term reliance on welfare benefits has normalized dependency. Many welfare recipients structure their lives around maximizing entitlements, seeing benefits not as temporary assistance but as guaranteed income.
- Generous government programs, including subsidized housing, free healthcare, and unemployment allowances, reduce the incentive to pursue formal employment.

**3. Multi-Generational Dependency:**

- Dependency on social benefits often becomes generational. Families who rely on welfare pass this lifestyle down to their children, creating a cycle of entitlement and poverty.

# The Education System: Degrees Without Opportunity

Publicly funded education systems, while intended to promote upward mobility, can unintentionally create a class of "professional students" who pursue multiple degrees without gaining real-world experience. Many students remain in school into their late twenties or thirties, not out of academic ambition, but because of the economic benefits attached to being a student.

Key Observations:

## 1. The "Eternal Student" Phenomenon:

- Many individuals stay enrolled in universities to maintain eligibility for student grants, housing subsidies, and healthcare coverage.
- Degrees become less about career advancement and more about sustaining government-supported lifestyles.

## 2. Unemployment Experts:

- Some individuals work only long enough to qualify for unemployment benefits, then quit their jobs and live on unemployment payouts.
- In certain European countries, individuals even migrate temporarily to work in another country, collect unemployment benefits there, and return to their home country to repeat the cycle.

## 3. Overqualified, Underemployed:

- A surplus of university graduates with degrees in non-marketable fields leads to underemployment.
- Governments often create low-paying public-sector jobs to absorb unemployed graduates, further straining state budgets while offering little economic return.

# The Myth Of "Free" Services

Public healthcare and education are often advertised as "free," creating the illusion that they come at no cost to the individual. In reality, these services are funded through high taxes and indirect contributions that disproportionately affect the working middle class.

Economic Realities:

**1. High Tax Burden:**

- Citizens in countries with extensive welfare systems face some of the world's highest tax rates, often exceeding 50% of income when combined with VAT, property taxes, and social contributions.

**2. Reduced Disposable Income:**

- After taxes, working individuals have limited disposable income, reducing their ability to save, invest, or start businesses.

**3. Public Services with Private Costs:**

- Even with universal healthcare, patients frequently face out-of-pocket expenses for medications, private specialists, and elective procedures.
- Parents often supplement "free" education with private tutoring and after-school programs due to declining public school quality.

# The Social Consequences

## Dependency and Lost Potential

The unintended social consequences of generous public welfare systems extend far beyond individual dependency. They shape societal behavior, undermine the work ethic, and contribute to economic stagnation.

Observed Social Trends:

**1. Erosion of Work Ethic:**

- Generous welfare benefits reduce the motivation to work, leading to widespread acceptance of non-participation in the labor market.
- Employers face a shrinking pool of motivated, skilled workers, resulting in labor shortages in critical industries.

**2. Decline in National Productivity:**

- High taxes and regulatory burdens drive entrepreneurs and skilled professionals to seek better opportunities abroad, weakening the domestic economy.
- Businesses are discouraged from expanding due to high labor costs, creating a stagnant economic environment.

**3. Political Instability and Populism:**

- Public dissatisfaction with economic stagnation, rising taxes, and growing welfare rolls contributes to political unrest.
- Populist parties often exploit these frustrations by promising sweeping welfare reforms, further polarizing societies.

## A Broken Social Contract

The original intent of public healthcare and education systems was to provide universal access and reduce inequality. However, their implementation has led to unintended consequences that have damaged individual ambition, created dependency, and hindered economic progress. The underlying issue is not the concept of public welfare itself, but the lack of balance between social safety nets and personal responsibility.

# Case Study 1: The European Welfare Cycle

## The Scenario

Having lived in Europe, where the public sector dominates critical areas such as healthcare, education, and social welfare, I have witnessed how well-intentioned government programs can inadvertently create cycles of economic dependency and social stagnation. While public systems aim to reduce inequality and provide universal access to essential services, the unintended consequences often outweigh the intended benefits. A common trend emerges where individuals pursue multiple degrees, not driven by intellectual curiosity or career ambitions, but to maintain eligibility for government benefits such as housing stipends, healthcare coverage, and student subsidies.

## Economic Consequences

The Endless Student Cycle: Degrees as a Survival Strategy

**Reality:**

Many young Europeans, particularly in countries like France, Italy, and Spain, remain in the education system well into their late twenties or even thirties. Pursuing additional degrees becomes less about career development and more about maintaining eligibility for generous government programs.

**Why It Happens:**

- **Student Status Equals Benefits:** Government policies often link social benefits like healthcare, housing stipends, and transportation discounts to student enrollment status.
- **Limited Incentive to Enter the Workforce:** Students face little immediate pressure to enter the labor market, knowing they can extend their studies and continue receiving government

assistance.

- **Artificial Demand for Higher Education:** Universities become overcrowded, degree programs lose their value due to oversaturation, and job qualifications escalate unnecessarily.

**Real Impact:**

- **Devalued Degrees:** When everyone holds multiple degrees, the job market becomes oversaturated, diminishing the value of academic qualifications.
- **Skill Gaps:** Continuous academic pursuits delay the development of real-world job skills and workplace experience.
- **Generational Dependency:** Entire generations become accustomed to relying on state-funded support rather than seeking economic independence.

## 2. High Taxes, Low Wages - The Employment Trap

**Reality:**

Even after graduation, young professionals face harsh economic conditions characterized by high taxes, government-mandated benefits, and limited opportunities for competitive, full-time employment.

**Why It Happens:**

- **High Tax Burden:** Countries with extensive social welfare programs impose heavy taxes on both individuals and businesses. Marginal tax rates on income can reach 50% or higher in nations like France, Denmark, and Sweden.
- **Employer Reluctance:** Strict labor regulations, such as mandatory paid leave, employer social contributions, and job security laws, discourage companies from hiring full-time employees.
- **Rise of Temporary Contracts:** Businesses increasingly opt for short-term contracts or freelance agreements to avoid the long-term costs associated with full-time hires.

**Real Impact:**

- **Underemployment:** Young graduates often settle for part-time or temporary work, unable to secure stable, well-paying jobs.
- **Reduced Disposable Income:** After taxes and mandatory contributions, many workers have minimal take-home pay, further discouraging economic ambition.
- **Social Resentment:** Frustration grows among hard-working professionals who see minimal reward for their labor, fostering disillusionment and a lack of motivation.

## 3. Brain Drain And Emigration - The Talent Exodus

**Reality:**

Faced with limited career prospects, low wages, and an oppressive tax burden, many skilled professionals seek better opportunities abroad.

**Why It Happens:**

- **Better Job Markets Elsewhere:** Countries with business-friendly environments, such as the United States, Canada, and Switzerland, attract European talent by offering lower tax rates, higher salaries, and a culture of entrepreneurship.
- **Stifled Entrepreneurship:** High start-up costs, heavy regulatory oversight, and high corporate taxes stifle entrepreneurship, driving ambitious individuals to more business-friendly economies.
- **Perpetuating the Cycle:** As talent leaves, the local economy suffers from a shrinking skilled workforce, making it even harder for businesses to thrive or expand.

**Real Impact:**

- **Economic Decline:** Countries lose their most promising minds, weakening their economic potential and technological competitiveness.

- **Demographic Crisis:** Aging populations left behind place further strain on the welfare state, requiring even higher taxes on a shrinking labor force.
- **Social Decline:** Families are separated as younger generations move abroad, creating fragmented societies with weakened community ties.

## Real-World Example: France's Labor Market Challenges

### Self-Employment Restrictions:

- The micro-entrepreneur status in France provides a simplified framework for small businesses, with specific annual revenue thresholds:
- €188,700 for commercial activities (e.g., sale of goods)
- €77,700 for service-based activities
- Exceeding these thresholds requires transitioning to a more complex business structure, such as a Société à Responsabilité Limitée (SARL), which involves additional administrative responsibilities and potential tax implications.

### Employer Social Contributions:

- Employers in France are subject to substantial social security contributions, averaging around 45% of an employee's gross salary.
- This high rate can deter hiring, leading businesses to favor part-time contracts or limit expansion to manage labor costs effectively.

### Youth Unemployment:

- France's youth unemployment rate remains elevated, partly due to rigid labor laws and employment protections that make employers hesitant to hire young, inexperienced workers.

- These regulations create barriers to entry for youth seeking employment, contributing to higher unemployment rates within this demographic.

## Concluding Insights

The European welfare cycle demonstrates how well-intentioned social policies can create counterproductive economic consequences. By tying social benefits to student status and imposing heavy taxes on businesses, these systems inadvertently reward dependency while discouraging economic self-sufficiency. In a cycle driven by high taxes, limited job prospects, and an exodus of talent, welfare states risk long-term stagnation and decline.

## Policy Recommendations:

1. **Promote Entrepreneurship:** Lower corporate taxes and reduce administrative barriers for startups and small businesses.
2. **Encourage Workforce Participation:** Adjust welfare eligibility to incentivize real employment rather than academic enrollment.
3. **Reduce Labor Market Regulations:** Make hiring and firing processes more flexible, allowing businesses to scale without fear of excessive costs.
4. **Lower Tax Burdens:** Reducing taxes on income and businesses would boost investment, job creation, and economic growth.

Without meaningful reforms, the European welfare model will continue trapping its citizens in a cycle of economic dependency, stagnation, and disillusionment. Only by embracing free-market principles, individual responsibility, and reduced government interference can Europe escape the welfare trap and restore economic vitality.

# Case Study 2 Healthcare Realities In Public Systems

## The Scenario:

Public healthcare systems in many European countries, such as the UK, France, and Spain, are built on the principle of universal access and minimal out-of-pocket expenses. While these systems offer competent care for common illnesses and preventive services, they struggle with significant delays in specialized and emergency care. As a result, many medical specialists leave public hospitals to establish private clinics, creating a two-tier healthcare system where only those with private insurance or cash can access timely, high-quality care.

## Economic Consequences

Service Delays: Overcrowded Public Hospitals

## Reality:

Public hospitals are consistently overwhelmed due to universal, low-cost access that encourages overutilization of healthcare services. Patients with non-urgent conditions often clog the system, leaving critical care patients facing long wait times for specialized treatments like surgeries, cancer therapies, and advanced diagnostics.

## Why It Happens:

- **Open Access Model:** Universal healthcare offers nearly free medical care, increasing patient demand far beyond the system's capacity.
- **Resource Limitations:** Staffing shortages, limited hospital beds, and outdated infrastructure prevent efficient patient care.
- **Bureaucratic Red Tape:** Resource allocation decisions often require multiple layers of government approval, delaying essential services.

**Real Impact:**

**Long Wait Times:** Elective surgeries can be delayed by months or even years. In countries like the UK (NHS), patients frequently wait over 12 months for non-urgent surgeries like hip replacements or cataract procedures.

**Routine vs. Critical Care Disparity:** Routine care such as check-ups and vaccinations is often efficient, but life-threatening conditions, including heart disease and cancer, face significant delays due to limited access to specialists.

**Patient Suffering:** The inability to receive timely treatment leads to worsening health conditions, diminished quality of life, and preventable fatalities.

# Specialist Exodus: A Brain Drain In Healthcare

**Reality:**
Highly trained specialists such as surgeons, oncologists, and cardiologists frequently leave public healthcare systems due to low government-mandated reimbursement rates and restrictive employment contracts. They open private clinics where they can charge market-based fees, often out of reach for the average citizen.

**Why It Happens:**

- **Low Reimbursement Rates:** Public healthcare systems often reimburse specialists at significantly lower rates compared to private insurance, making public sector work financially unsustainable.
- **Career Limitations:** Public healthcare employment often comes with rigid pay scales, bureaucratic interference, and limited opportunities for professional growth.
- **Administrative Burdens:** Doctors in public systems must comply with excessive paperwork, performance quotas, and bureaucratic policies that limit their ability to deliver personalized care.

**Real Impact:**

- **Two-Tier System:** Patients with private insurance or the ability to pay cash enjoy shorter wait times and superior care in private clinics.
- **Limited Specialist Availability:** Those relying solely on public healthcare are left competing for limited specialist appointments, extending wait times for even urgent care services.
- **Reduced System Capacity:** Public healthcare systems lose many of their best specialists, weakening their ability to provide advanced care.

# Medical Tourism: Escaping The System

**Reality:**
Frustrated by long wait times and limited access to life-saving procedures, many patients choose to travel abroad to countries with better healthcare infrastructure, lower costs, and shorter queues. This has led to the rise of a global medical tourism industry that siphons both money and medical expertise from home countries.

**Why It Happens:**

- **Affordable Alternatives:** Countries like India, Thailand, and Mexico have become popular destinations for affordable, high-quality medical procedures such as orthopedic surgeries, cardiac operations, and cosmetic procedures.
- **Reduced Bureaucracy:** Private clinics abroad offer faster service, fewer bureaucratic hurdles, and personalized care.
- **Insurance Gaps:** Many public healthcare systems only cover in-country care, forcing patients to pay out-of-pocket for overseas treatment.

**Real Impact:**

- **Economic Drain:** Money spent abroad weakens the home country's economy and healthcare system, diverting resources that could otherwise improve domestic healthcare infrastructure.
- **Talent Migration:** Successful foreign clinics often attract highly skilled doctors from public systems, contributing to a worsening "brain drain."
- **Risk of Complications:** Patients may face medical complications after returning home, requiring emergency care in already overburdened public hospitals.

# Hidden Costs: The Myth Of "Free" Healthcare

**Reality:**

Public healthcare systems are often advertised as "free," creating the illusion of universal, no-cost care. In practice, patients still face numerous hidden expenses, such as co-payments for medications, transportation fees, supplemental insurance costs, and long-term care services.

**Why It Happens:**

**Co-Payments and Deductibles:** Patients in countries like France and Germany often pay out-of-pocket for prescription drugs, medical devices, and specialized therapies.

**Supplemental Insurance Requirements:** In systems like France's Sécurité Sociale, basic public healthcare covers only a percentage of medical expenses. Citizens must purchase private "top-up" insurance to cover the rest, creating additional financial burdens.

**Non-Medical Expenses:** Travel costs, child care during hospital visits, and lost income due to lengthy wait times add to patients' out-of-pocket expenses.

**Real Impact:**

**Financial Hardship:** While the wealthy can afford private insurance and specialized care, low-income individuals often face serious economic hardships when public healthcare fails to deliver timely or adequate services.

**Widening Socioeconomic Gap:** The disparity in care creates a system where wealth determines access to life-saving treatments.

**Patient Frustration:** The gap between public promises and real-world experiences leads to widespread dissatisfaction with public healthcare systems.

## The False Promise Of Public Healthcare

Despite being portrayed as models of equality and fairness, public healthcare systems in many European countries reveal deep flaws. Overburdened hospitals, delayed treatment, and a critical shortage of specialists create a divided healthcare landscape where only the wealthy can access timely, high-quality care. Government-imposed reimbursement rates and rigid regulations discourage medical innovation while forcing talented doctors to seek better-paying jobs abroad or in the private sector.

The result is a healthcare system that fails to live up to its promises, leaving millions trapped in a cycle of dependency, delay, and despair. Meaningful reform would require decentralizing healthcare management, encouraging private sector competition, and introducing market-based solutions that reward efficiency, innovation, and exceptional care. Only through reducing bureaucratic control and empowering both patients and providers can public healthcare systems avoid collapse and deliver on their intended purpose—true, equitable healthcare for all.

# Case Study 3: Tax Burden And Middle-Class Erosion

### The Scenario:

European-style welfare systems rely on high taxes to sustain extensive public services, including universal healthcare, free education, and social welfare programs. While these systems promise social equality and security, they impose a severe tax burden on the middle class. The economic consequences include diminished economic mobility, stifled entrepreneurship, and reduced incentives for investment. The result is a shrinking middle class trapped between high taxes and limited upward mobility, while wealth accumulation becomes increasingly difficult.

### Economic Consequences

### 1. Progressive Tax Systems: Crushing the Middle Class

### Reality:

Middle-class workers in many European countries face

progressive tax systems with combined income, sales, and property tax rates ranging from **40% to 60% or more**. In nations like Sweden, Denmark, and France, even average earners fall into high tax brackets, reducing disposable income and making wealth accumulation nearly impossible.

**Why It Happens:**

- **High Marginal Tax Rates:** Income tax rates in countries like Sweden reach **57%** for middle- to high-income earners, while France imposes income tax rates up to **45%**, not including social security contributions.
- **Social Contributions:** On top of income taxes, workers contribute significant amounts to social security programs such as healthcare, pensions, and unemployment insurance, further reducing take-home pay.
- **Indirect Taxes:** Value-Added Tax (VAT) rates in the European Union average **20% to 25%**, taxing everyday purchases and driving up the cost of living.

**Real Impact:**

- **Diminished Disposable Income:** After taxes, most middle-class families struggle to save, invest, or afford private services like supplemental health insurance or better education.
- **Wealth Stagnation:** Without the ability to accumulate savings or build assets like property or investments, middle-class families find themselves stuck in an economic cycle with limited upward mobility.
- **Debt Reliance:** Many resort to personal loans and credit to cover essential expenses, trapping them in long-term debt.

## 2. Discouraged Entrepreneurship: Stifling Innovation

**Reality:**

Europe's high taxes and strict regulations discourage entrepreneurship and small business creation. Aspiring entrepreneurs face steep start-up costs, complex tax codes, and excessive bureaucratic oversight, making risk-taking economically unfeasible.

**Why It Happens:**

**Corporate Tax Rates:** Countries like France impose corporate tax rates as high as **25% to 33%**, alongside employer-paid social security contributions of **45% to 60%** of employee salaries.

**Bureaucratic Red Tape:** Business owners must navigate extensive regulatory requirements, including business registration, tax filings, environmental compliance, and labor law adherence.

**Hiring Restrictions:** Rigid labor laws make firing employees costly and legally challenging, discouraging job creation and limiting a business's ability to adapt.

**Real Impact:**

**Business Flight:** Many entrepreneurs relocate to more business-friendly countries like the U.S., the U.K., or Switzerland, resulting in an economic "brain drain."

**Limited Economic Growth:** With fewer businesses being established, job creation slows, and economies become increasingly reliant on state-funded programs to generate employment.

**Informal Economy Growth:** High tax rates incentivize informal or "black market" business activities to avoid taxation, reducing overall government revenue.

## 3. Welfare Dependency: Disincentivizing Work

**Reality:**

Generous social welfare programs, including unemployment benefits, child allowances, and housing subsidies, can create a system where remaining on government assistance is financially more advantageous than working. This discourages job-seeking and reduces labor force participation.

**Why It Happens:**

**High Welfare Payments:** In some countries, unemployment benefits can equal or exceed the wages offered by low-skilled jobs, reducing the incentive to seek employment.

**Benefit Cliffs:** Income thresholds for receiving welfare benefits can create "cliffs," where earning slightly more disqualifies individuals from essential assistance, discouraging career advancement.

**Cultural Shift:** A multi-generational culture of welfare dependency can emerge, with children raised in households reliant on government support often repeating the same cycle.

**Real Impact:**

**Labor Shortages:** Low-skilled job sectors such as hospitality, retail, and agriculture often face labor shortages because available jobs pay less than state-funded assistance.

**Reduced Productivity:** With fewer people participating in the labor force, national productivity declines, slowing economic growth and reducing the tax base needed to sustain welfare programs.

**Economic Inefficiency:** Governments are forced to raise taxes further to fund expanding welfare programs, exacerbating the economic strain on middle-class taxpayers.

## Real-World Examples

**France's Tax Burden Example:**

**Income and Social Taxes:** French workers contribute up to **45%** in income tax and an additional **15% to 20%** in social security contributions, totaling a tax burden of over **60%** in some cases.

**Wealth Tax History:** France's former "Wealth Tax" targeted individuals with significant assets, driving thousands of wealthy citizens and entrepreneurs out of the country.

The government eventually repealed it due to its adverse economic impact.

**Entrepreneurial Exodus:** France has experienced a notable exodus of entrepreneurs to countries like the U.K. and the U.S., where business environments are more favorable.

**Sweden's High Tax Model:**

**Progressive Tax Rates:** In Sweden, high-income earners face income tax rates exceeding **57%**, plus a **25% VAT** on goods and services.

**Social Benefits vs. Wealth Accumulation:** While Sweden's social benefits are extensive, its tax rates make it difficult for middle-class families to build wealth or invest in businesses.

## The Tax Trap And Middle-Class Erosion

The European welfare model, while promoting social equality and universal services, imposes a crushing tax burden that disproportionately affects the middle class. Far from leveling the playing field, progressive tax systems, rigid labor laws, and extensive welfare programs create a vicious cycle of dependency, economic stagnation, and reduced upward mobility.

Middle-class families pay the highest price, caught between excessive taxes and limited access to private services. Without the ability to save, invest, or build businesses, they face restricted financial independence and generational wealth stagnation. Entrepreneurs and skilled professionals leave for more business-friendly countries, further weakening the economic base.

To break this cycle, welfare-dependent economies must reduce tax rates, simplify business regulations, and incentivize entrepreneurship. By fostering economic freedom and encouraging personal responsibility, nations can empower individuals to succeed—creating a sustainable economic future built on growth, innovation, and reduced dependency on state-funded programs.

# Case Study 4:Healthcare Realities In The U.s.

*Introduction of the ACA*

The Affordable Care Act (ACA), signed into law in 2010, fundamentally reshaped the U.S. healthcare system by expanding government control over insurance markets and mandating coverage. While the ACA aimed to provide universal healthcare access, it inadvertently created a two-tier system. Public insurance programs like Medicaid expanded, while rising premiums and reduced insurance options drove many Americans to pay out-of-pocket for private healthcare services.

## Economic Consequences
Overburdened Public Healthcare Networks

## Reality:
The ACA led to an influx of previously uninsured patients entering the healthcare system, overwhelming public clinics and hospitals. While Medicaid expansion extended coverage, it strained the capacity of providers who were already managing heavy patient loads.

## Why It Happened:

- **Medicaid Expansion:** Millions gained insurance through Medicaid, but reimbursement rates for providers remained low, discouraging specialists from accepting Medicaid patients.
- **Provider Shortages:** A growing number of doctors opted out of public insurance networks, reducing the number of available providers.

## Real Impact:

- **Long Wait Times:** Publicly insured patients often face delays of several months for specialist appointments, similar to public healthcare systems in Europe.
- **Emergency Room Overload:** Many patients unable to access

timely care resort to emergency rooms, further burdening hospitals and inflating healthcare costs.

## Specialist Exodus and Decline in Participation

**Reality:**

The ACA imposed government-set reimbursement rates that were often too low to sustain medical practices, prompting many specialists to limit or refuse Medicaid and Medicare patients.

**Why It Happened:**

- **Reduced Profit Margins:** With capped reimbursements and complex billing regulations, specialists found private practice more lucrative.
- **Private Clinics Thrive:** Specialists increasingly set up concierge or cash-based clinics, offering premium services outside of insurance networks.

**Real Impact:**

- **Two-Tier System:** Wealthier patients who can afford private care enjoy faster, higher-quality service, while low-income patients are confined to overburdened public systems.
- **Access Gaps:** Critical specialties like oncology, cardiology, and orthopedics experience significant provider shortages within the public network.

## Medical Tourism: A Growing U.S. Trend

**Reality:**

Frustrated by limited access and rising costs, many Americans travel abroad for medical procedures, seeking lower-cost treatments and shorter wait times.

**Why It Happened:**

- **Rising Premiums:** The ACA's essential health benefits and coverage mandates drove up premiums for many middle-class families.

**Limited Provider Networks:** Insurance plans under the ACA often feature narrow networks, forcing patients to seek alternative care outside the U.S.

## Real Impact:

**Economic Drain:** Money that could be reinvested in the U.S. healthcare system instead flows to medical hubs abroad, such as Mexico, India, and Thailand.

**Quality Disparities:** Patients face varying care quality abroad, with some experiencing life-threatening complications after surgeries performed outside the U.S.

# The Myth Of "Affordable" Care

## Reality:

While the ACA promised affordable care, many Americans experienced rising premiums, high deductibles, and limited coverage. For those who qualified for subsidies, hidden costs remained unavoidable.

## Why It Happened:

**Mandated Coverage:** The ACA forced insurers to cover a broad range of services, raising the cost of insurance plans.

**Co-Payments and Deductibles:** Even insured patients face high out-of-pocket expenses due to soaring deductibles and required co-payments.

## Real Impact:

**Middle-Class Squeeze:** Families earning above subsidy eligibility thresholds often pay thousands annually in premiums, plus out-of-pocket expenses.

**Economic Inequality:** Wealthy Americans can bypass the system by paying cash, while low-income Americans rely on strained public programs—leaving the middle class stuck with high costs and limited care options.

# A Broken Promise Of Affordable Care

The ACA, intended to equalize access to healthcare, has produced an increasingly divided system similar to Europe's public-private healthcare divide. Government regulations, capped reimbursements, and expanding public insurance rolls have weakened the quality of care for millions while driving up costs. Patients face long wait times, limited access to specialists, and inflated premiums that strain household budgets.

A sustainable healthcare system requires less government control, competitive free-market reforms, and reduced regulatory burdens on providers. Restoring healthcare freedom through price transparency, expanded health savings accounts (HSAs), and broader insurance competition would return decision-making power to patients and providers—breaking the cycle of dependency and inefficiency created by government overreach.

# Broader Impacts And Policy Failures

The promises of public healthcare and education systems often mask deeply entrenched failures rooted in poor policy design, mismanagement, and corrupt practices. While these systems claim to reduce inequality and promote economic stability, their real-world consequences reveal widespread economic stagnation, rampant corruption, and worsening social divides. The following sections explore the damaging realities behind government-run systems.

# Economic Stagnation

Public funding models based on high taxation often limit economic growth by reducing disposable income, discouraging investment, and stifling job creation.

**Key Failures:**

**Crippling Tax Burden:**

In countries with expansive welfare programs, individuals frequently lose 40% to 60% of their income through various taxes, including income, sales, and social security contributions.

Entrepreneurs face suffocating tax obligations, discouraging business expansion and innovation.

**Disincentive to Work:**

Extensive welfare programs encourage reliance on state benefits rather than job-seeking.

Citizens often calculate that living on government assistance provides a comparable standard of living to working full-time, leading to widespread welfare dependency.

**Investment Exodus:**

Businesses flee high-tax countries, moving operations to regions with friendlier tax policies.

Capital flight leads to long-term underdevelopment, job losses, and reduced national competitiveness.

**Underdeveloped Private Sector:**

In welfare-heavy economies, the state becomes the largest employer, dominating entire sectors.

A lack of competition creates stagnation, leaving public services inefficient, underfunded, and resistant to reform.

## Political Corruption And Waste

Government-run systems breed mismanagement, fraud, and nepotism through lack of accountability, opaque budgets, and entrenched political interests.

**Key Failures:**

**Budget Mismanagement:**

Massive public budgets are allocated through complicated processes shielded from public scrutiny.

Frequent overspending and budget deficits become routine, financed by higher taxes or national debt.

**Crony Capitalism:**

Government contracts are awarded based on political loyalty, bribery, or nepotism rather than merit or cost-efficiency.

Entire industries become reliant on government favoritism, fostering corruption at all administrative levels.

**Pharmaceutical Lobbying:**

In public healthcare, large pharmaceutical companies influence policy to favor long-term treatment plans over actual cures, keeping patients dependent on costly medications.

Politicians and health officials often benefit from lobbying, while the public suffers from overpriced and ineffective healthcare solutions.

**Educational Lobbying and Union Power:**

Teachers' unions protect underperforming educators and block meaningful reforms in public education.

Politicians frequently trade education funding for electoral support from powerful unions, leaving students with outdated curricula and failing schools.


## Social Stratification

Despite claims of equality, government-controlled systems widen social inequalities by reserving high-quality services for the wealthy and leaving the poor dependent on failing public institutions.

**Key Failures:**

**Two-Tier Healthcare Systems:**

While public healthcare is presented as universal, long wait times and limited access force those who can afford it to seek private care.

Private insurance and out-of-pocket payments create a parallel system, leaving the poorest citizens stuck in overcrowded, underfunded hospitals.

**Education for the Elite:**

Wealthy families supplement "free" public education with private tutoring, elite schools, and international universities.

Poorer families remain trapped in failing public schools, limiting upward mobility and reinforcing generational poverty.

**Housing Inequality:**

Government-subsidized housing is often allocated through corrupt bureaucratic processes, leaving many deserving families without adequate shelter.

The wealthy bypass the system entirely by purchasing luxury homes, further widening the housing gap.

**Political Elite Privilege:**

Politicians advocating for public healthcare and education frequently avoid these services themselves, enrolling their children in elite private schools and receiving top-tier private medical care.

This hypocrisy underscores the system's inherent inequality, as public services become the default only for those unable to afford better options.

**Chapter 3**

# SOCIAL AND POLITICAL CONSEQUENCES

## Impacts On Citizens, Access, And Quality.

Public healthcare, education, and economic policies, though designed to create equitable societies, often produce the opposite effect. Instead of ensuring fairness and universal access, these state-managed systems frequently devolve into bureaucratic juggernauts marked by overregulation, oppressive taxation, and expanding government control. The result is a cycle of dependency, economic stagnation, and diminished personal freedoms.

### Economic Constraints and Bureaucratic Overreach

Small businesses, the engine of economic growth, struggle under excessive taxes and complex compliance mandates. Complex regulatory frameworks favor well-connected corporations that can absorb the administrative expenses while crushing emerging entrepreneurs. This results in reduced market competition, fewer job opportunities, and a monopolistic environment where corporate lobbying replaces fair competition.

Meanwhile, individuals experience limited economic mobility due to burdensome taxes that erode disposable income. As social welfare systems expand, citizens are trapped in a cycle where government dependency is often more financially secure than striving for personal success. Tax-funded programs become lifelines, discouraging initiative and creating a welfare state that penalizes productivity and rewards passive dependence.

**Political Exploitation and Institutional Corruption**

Government-managed systems inevitably attract political exploitation. Public contracts are awarded not based on merit or efficiency but through political favoritism and crony capitalism. Politicians offer lucrative deals to supportive corporations while using social welfare promises to secure votes. Corruption festers within this system, with public funds misallocated to pet projects designed to enhance political power rather than public welfare.

Powerful elites, shielded by privilege and access, manipulate these systems for personal gain while imposing regulations that restrict the very people they claim to serve. The same politicians advocating for "fairness" often create policies that shield themselves from the burdens they impose on ordinary citizens.

**Social Decline Through Dependency and Resentment**

State-managed systems also shape societal attitudes. Over time, dependence on government services breeds complacency, reducing the incentive to pursue self-reliance, innovation, or economic advancement. Citizens become conditioned to expect state assistance, fostering a culture of entitlement that erodes personal responsibility. The resulting stagnation limits social progress and deepens economic divides.

At the same time, resentment grows among taxpayers who see their hard-earned money funneled into inefficient programs and corrupt initiatives. This fuels political polarization, social unrest, and a deepening divide between those who benefit from government favoritism and those burdened by its inefficiencies.

# Economic Suppression Through Taxation And Regulation

## Case Study: France's Punitive Tax System

A close friend of mine runs a construction business in the south of France, specializing in home improvement projects like building verandas, installing windows, and general renovations. Despite his success, government-imposed revenue caps and steep taxes create major obstacles to growing his business.

France's complex tax and regulatory framework poses significant challenges for small business owners, particularly those operating under the micro-entrepreneur status. While this system was designed to simplify business operations for sole proprietors, its strict revenue limits and administrative burdens restrict business growth and discourage expansion.

### Revenue Cap Restrictions

**Turnover Limits:**
Micro-entrepreneurs face strict annual revenue ceilings:

- **€176,200** for commercial activities like selling goods and home construction.
- **€72,600** for service-based businesses such as consulting or repair services.

These caps limit how much revenue a small business can generate before being forced into a more complex and costly business structure.

**Transition to SARL (Société à Responsabilité Limitée):**

Exceeding these thresholds requires transitioning to a **SARL (Limited Liability Company)**, triggering extensive administrative responsibilities such as:

- **Comprehensive Accounting:** Full financial statements must be prepared and audited.
- **Corporate Taxes:** Businesses become subject to higher corporate tax rates.
- **Business Insurance:** Mandatory business liability insurance becomes an additional fixed expense.

**Real-World Impact:**

This policy forces small businesses into a difficult choice: either limit growth to remain within the micro-entrepreneur tax bracket or register as a SARL and face skyrocketing costs. Many entrepreneurs choose to remain small or even underreport revenue to avoid these burdens.

## Employer Taxes And Social Contributions

**Employer Contributions:**

France's social security contributions are among the highest in the world. Employers must contribute up to **45% to 60%** of each employee's gross salary toward mandatory programs such as:

- **Health Insurance**
- **Unemployment Insurance**
- **State Pensions**
- **Family Allowances**

These contributions significantly raise payroll costs, making hiring full-time employees prohibitively expensive for small businesses.

**Impact on Hiring:**

- **Job Market Distortion:** High payroll taxes discourage hiring, forcing many small businesses to rely on part-time or temporary workers.

- **Informal Labor Dependence:** Some business owners resort to hiring informal or under-the-table workers to avoid excessive employer contributions, risking legal and financial penalties.
- **Limited Business Expansion:** The inability to scale operations due to labor costs forces many small businesses to remain one-person operations.

## Regulatory Burden

**Labor Laws:**
French labor laws offer some of the world's most generous worker protections, including:

- **Minimum Paid Leave:** Workers receive a minimum of **five weeks of paid vacation annually**, plus numerous public holidays.
- **Severance Packages:** Employers must provide legally mandated severance pay, even in cases of business closure.
- **Job Security Protections:** Strict labor laws make dismissing an underperforming employee legally complex and costly, often involving court proceedings and significant payouts.

**Administrative Requirements:**
Small businesses operating under the micro-entrepreneur status must comply with various administrative rules, including:

- **Revenue and Expense Tracking:** Every business transaction must be logged, and records must be preserved for **up to 10 years**.
- **Compliance Inspections:** Government agencies frequently conduct inspections, imposing fines for any regulatory infractions.

**Real-World Impact:**
These regulations often force business owners to spend more time managing compliance than growing their businesses. The constant threat of inspections and legal disputes creates an atmosphere of uncertainty and discourages risk-taking.

## A System That Punishes Success

France's high-tax, highly regulated business environment creates a hostile landscape for entrepreneurs. Revenue caps, steep employer contributions, and rigid labor laws work together to suppress business expansion and deter investment.

Small business owners must operate within an inflexible system that penalizes growth and rewards staying small or underreporting income. Many skilled entrepreneurs, including my friend, are left with few options: remain limited, navigate an impossible bureaucratic maze, or relocate to a more business-friendly country.

To encourage entrepreneurship and economic vitality, meaningful reforms are essential. These include reducing employer contributions, raising revenue caps, simplifying business registration processes, and introducing more flexible labor laws. Only by addressing these structural issues can France unlock its entrepreneurial potential and create a truly dynamic, competitive economy.

## Social Consequences Of Government Overreach

*Lessons from France's Regulatory Trap*

Government overreach, excessive taxation, and regulatory red tape have far-reaching social consequences that extend beyond economic stagnation. Drawing parallels from France's punitive tax and business policies, similar dynamics are increasingly visible in the United States. The erosion of entrepreneurship, shrinking middle class, and growing welfare dependency highlight how unchecked government intervention can reshape the socioeconomic fabric of a nation.

## Discouraged Entrepreneurship

**Excessive Regulation and Tax Burden:**

Much like France's restrictive business environment, small business owners in the U.S. face burdensome regulations, excessive taxes, and steep compliance costs. The rise of state-mandated minimum wages, employer healthcare mandates under the Affordable Care Act (ACA), and federal payroll taxes discourages many from formally registering businesses or expanding their operations.

**Real-World Impact:**

- **Shadow Economy Expansion:** Many aspiring entrepreneurs avoid business registration altogether, opting to operate in the informal sector. This underground economy deprives the government of taxable revenue while exposing informal workers to wage theft, unsafe working conditions, and limited legal protection.
- **Entrepreneurial Exodus:** Ambitious business owners often move to more business-friendly states or countries with lower taxes and fewer regulations, further weakening local economies.

**Case Comparison - USA and France:**

- **France's Tax Pressure:** Micro-entrepreneurs in France are frequently forced to underreport earnings to avoid surpassing revenue thresholds, triggering higher tax brackets and mandatory business structure changes like registering as a SARL. This practice stems from a complex tax system designed to target growing businesses, penalizing success rather than encouraging expansion.
- **U.S. Tax Burden:** In the United States, business owners face

similarly restrictive tax policies. While the federal corporate tax rate is capped at 21%, additional state and local business taxes, payroll contributions, and compliance costs often push the total tax burden much higher. Complicated IRS regulations further discourage entrepreneurship by imposing extensive filing requirements, tax audits, and penalty risks, creating a hostile environment for small business growth.

## Stagnant Middle Class

**Wealth Suppression through Over-Taxation:**

Much like in France, where high taxation prevents small businesses from accumulating wealth, U.S. middle-class entrepreneurs face similar struggles. Rising tax rates, increased costs of living, and healthcare expenses prevent individuals from building lasting financial security.

**Real-World Impact:**

- **Limited Economic Mobility:** The tax burden on small businesses and middle-income families means that even moderate financial success can result in higher tax brackets, reducing disposable income and limiting investment in education, housing, or retirement.
- **Decline of Family-Owned Businesses:** Family-run businesses that form the backbone of the U.S. middle class face overwhelming tax liabilities upon succession, often leading to closures rather than generational wealth transfer.

**Case Comparison - USA and France:**

**Social Security and Medicare Taxes:** U.S. business owners must contribute to payroll taxes for Social Security and Medicare, similar to France's high employer contributions. Combined with income taxes, this suppresses upward mobility for entrepreneurs.

**Inflation and Debt:** Rising inflation, stagnant wages, and student loan debt further weaken the U.S. middle class, mirroring France's stagnant economic environment caused by high taxes and strict labor laws.

## Social Welfare Dependence

### Collapse of Small Businesses:

When small businesses collapse due to overwhelming tax burdens and regulatory obstacles, displaced workers are left with few alternatives but to rely on government assistance programs such as unemployment benefits, food stamps, and Medicaid. The government must expand social spending to accommodate this growing dependency, further exacerbating the national debt.

### Real-World Impact:

- **Welfare Dependency Cycle:** A significant portion of the U.S. population becomes reliant on government aid, creating a permanent welfare class with reduced incentives to re-enter the workforce.
- **Disincentive to Work:** Welfare programs often create income cliffs, where earning even slightly more disqualifies recipients from critical benefits, discouraging work and career advancement.

### Case Comparison - USA and France:

- **Social Benefits Culture:** France's expansive social welfare system, funded by high taxes, has created a generational dependency on government support. Similarly, in the U.S., entitlement programs such as Medicaid and SNAP (Supplemental Nutrition Assistance Program) have expanded significantly, creating a politically charged debate over welfare reform.
- **Labor Shortages and Welfare Incentives:** During the COVID-19 pandemic, enhanced U.S. unemployment benefits discouraged many from returning to work, mirroring

France's welfare dependency issues driven by its generous unemployment policies.

## Broader Social Impacts

### Erosion of Individual Responsibility:
Government overreach often shifts societal attitudes, fostering reliance on state assistance instead of encouraging entrepreneurship and personal responsibility. In the U.S., as in France, this results in a cultural shift toward entitlement rather than self-sufficiency.

### Political Manipulation:
Expansive social welfare systems become powerful political tools, enabling politicians to secure votes through promises of increased social benefits. This creates an entrenched system where government dependency becomes politically incentivized.

### Social Frustration and Resentment:
Taxpayers who fund these programs often feel frustrated by perceived government inefficiency and misuse of public funds. In both the U.S. and France, this resentment fuels political polarization and social unrest.

### Generational Poverty:
Multi-generational reliance on welfare deepens poverty, creating a class of citizens permanently detached from the workforce. Poor education, lack of vocational training, and minimal financial literacy reinforce this cycle of poverty in both nations.

## The Need For Structural Reform

To break this cycle of social and economic stagnation,

comprehensive reform is needed:

**Lower Taxes for Entrepreneurs:** Reducing corporate and payroll taxes would encourage business creation, investment, and job growth.

**Deregulation of Small Businesses:** Simplifying tax codes and business registration processes would ease the administrative burden on entrepreneurs.

**Welfare Reform:** Welfare programs should be structured to incentivize work, education, and self-improvement, rather than fostering long-term dependency.

**Economic Incentive Policies:** Introducing tax breaks, low-interest loans, and grants for small businesses could stimulate innovation and economic expansion.

By limiting government overreach and promoting entrepreneurship, both the U.S. and France can restore social mobility, reduce dependency, and revitalize their economies. The key lies in balancing social welfare programs with policies that incentivize personal responsibility, economic opportunity, and long-term national prosperity.

# Political Consequences Of State-Driven Economies

When governments adopt state-driven economic models, centralizing control over major sectors like healthcare, education, and business regulation, they create unintended political consequences that destabilize societies and erode democratic institutions. These outcomes include expanding bureaucratic systems, deepening public disillusionment, and entrenching political privilege among elites.

## Expanding Bureaucracy

**Administrative Bloat:**
State-driven economies rely on expansive bureaucracies to

enforce regulations, manage public services, and distribute welfare benefits. This creates a complex web of government agencies staffed by career civil servants whose livelihoods depend on maintaining and expanding these systems.

**Endless Regulation:** As bureaucracies grow, they generate new rules, procedures, and compliance mandates to justify their existence, creating an overwhelming regulatory framework that stifles private-sector growth.

**Unaccountable Civil Servants:** Government officials often operate with minimal oversight, fostering an environment where incompetence, corruption, and inefficiency become routine.

**Corruption Networks:** In extreme cases, public officials extract bribes or grant special favors in return for business contracts, further undermining public trust in state institutions.

**Example:**

In countries like France, complex labor laws and tax codes require entire agencies dedicated to compliance enforcement, creating layers of government administration that complicate everyday business operations.

## Rise Of Populist Movements

**Economic Stagnation and Political Instability:**
State-driven economies often experience slow economic growth due to over-regulation, high taxation, and limited private-sector innovation. Citizens facing unemployment, reduced wages, and declining public services grow increasingly frustrated.

**Populist Uprisings:** Economic hardship fuels anti-establishment sentiment, prompting voters to support populist leaders who promise radical reforms, protectionist policies, or even nationalization of key industries.

**Political Polarization:** Populist rhetoric often divides societies into "elites" versus "the people," deepening social and political fractures.

**Authoritarian Drift:** In some cases, populist leaders consolidate power through emergency decrees, limiting civil liberties under the guise of restoring economic stability.

**Example:**

The "Yellow Vest" protests in France emerged from frustration over high taxes, stagnant wages, and worsening public services, reflecting a broader populist backlash against the political establishment.

# Elite Privilege And Government Hypocrisy

**Double Standards:**

While state-driven economies are promoted as tools for creating equality and fairness, political elites frequently bypass the very systems they manage. The ruling class often enjoys private services while enforcing reliance on public institutions for the general population.

**Exclusive Healthcare and Education:** Many politicians send their children to prestigious private schools and receive healthcare from elite private clinics while maintaining failing public systems for everyone else.

**Insulated from Consequences:** Political elites shield themselves from the hardships faced by ordinary citizens, ensuring that even severe economic downturns or policy failures rarely impact their privileged lifestyles.

**Example:**

In many state-driven economies, government officials are entitled to special health insurance plans, diplomatic passports, and access to international education networks— benefits unavailable to ordinary taxpayers funding the public system.

# Voter Disillusionment

**Loss of Public Trust:**
Citizens become disillusioned when political promises of reform and prosperity consistently fail due to corruption, incompetence, and corporate lobbying. Repeated policy failures erode trust in democratic institutions, making voters apathetic and disengaged.

- **Low Voter Turnout:** Widespread frustration leads to declining voter participation, undermining democratic accountability.
- **Entrenched Political Elites:** When voters disengage, corrupt politicians and ineffective bureaucrats remain in power through manipulation, political favoritism, and rigged electoral systems.
- **Political Apathy:** As hope for meaningful change diminishes, civil unrest becomes more likely, resulting in protests, strikes, and even violent uprisings.

**Example:**

In countries experiencing economic crises and persistent corruption, such as Venezuela or Greece, low voter turnout has allowed entrenched political parties to maintain power despite clear public dissatisfaction.

# A Cycle Of Political Decay

State-driven economies, by design, expand government power, creating a cycle where bloated bureaucracies, elite privilege, populist uprisings, and voter disillusionment reinforce one another. These consequences destabilize nations by fostering economic stagnation, weakening democratic institutions, and deepening social inequality. To break this cycle, governments must embrace policies that prioritize transparency, reduce bureaucratic overreach, and ensure that public officials are held accountable—restoring trust and empowering citizens rather than perpetuating government dependency.

# Access And Quality Gaps In Public Services

Public services such as healthcare, education, and infrastructure are intended to provide equal access to essential resources. However, government-run systems often struggle with unequal distribution, creating significant disparities between socioeconomic groups and geographic regions. These gaps reinforce social inequalities and reduce the effectiveness of public welfare programs.

# Healthcare Inequalities

**Systemic Shortcomings:**
Government-managed healthcare systems frequently experience critical failures such as long wait times, limited specialist availability, and uneven service quality. These challenges stem from underfunding, mismanagement, and rigid bureaucratic policies that restrict flexibility and innovation.

**Two-Tier System:**

- **Privileged Access:** Those who can afford private healthcare bypass the public system entirely, gaining faster, better-quality care.
- **Wealth-Driven Outcomes:** Access to life-saving treatments and advanced procedures often depends on an individual's ability to pay, creating a healthcare divide based on wealth rather than medical urgency.
- **Delayed Care:** Long wait times for diagnostics, surgeries, and specialist consultations lead to worsened health outcomes for those reliant on the public system.

**Real-World Example:**

In countries like the UK and Canada, national healthcare systems struggle with chronic delays for elective surgeries and specialist appointments, driving patients to seek private care despite high taxes funding the public system.

# Educational Disparities

**Public vs. Private Divide:**
While public education is theoretically free and universally accessible, the quality of education is often determined by geographic location and household income. Funding disparities between school districts create an uneven playing field where students from wealthier areas have access to better facilities, experienced teachers, and advanced programs.

**Parental Intervention:**

**Supplemental Education:** Wealthier families can afford private tutoring, extracurricular activities, and international school programs to fill gaps in the public system.

**Curriculum Inequities:** Underfunded public schools often lack up-to-date textbooks, STEM resources, and technology, leaving disadvantaged students far behind their peers.

**Cycle of Inequality:**

**Generational Impact:** Children from lower-income households frequently receive subpar education, limiting their future career prospects and reinforcing cycles of poverty.

**College Access:** Wealthier students are better positioned for college admission due to access to test preparation services, private schools, and personal networks.

**Real-World Example:**

In the U.S., property taxes fund public schools, creating vast funding differences between affluent suburbs and inner-city districts, perpetuating a system where zip code determines educational opportunity.

# Regional Disparities

**Rural Neglect:**

**Limited Services:** Rural areas often face critical shortages of healthcare providers, underfunded schools, and decaying infrastructure due to lower population densities and reduced tax revenue.

**Resource Scarcity:** Rural hospitals may lack advanced medical equipment, forcing residents to travel long distances for specialized care. Similarly, rural schools frequently struggle with teacher shortages and outdated facilities.

**Urban Overcrowding:**

**Strained Systems:** In contrast, urban centers, while better funded, face their own set of challenges, including overcrowded classrooms, congested hospitals, and bureaucratic inefficiencies that hinder service delivery.

**Social Fragmentation:** Wealthier urban residents may insulate themselves by using private hospitals and schools, further stretching public services for lower-income residents.

**Real-World Example:**

In countries like France and the U.S., healthcare and education quality drop significantly in rural regions compared to urban centers, where infrastructure investment is prioritized.


## A System Built On Inequities

Despite being designed to promote fairness and equality, public service systems often exacerbate social and economic divides. The inherent inefficiencies in government-managed healthcare and education create a reality where access and quality are dictated by geography and financial status. Without targeted reforms that address funding equity, transparency, and service accountability, these public systems will continue to fall short of their promises —reinforcing privilege for the few while leaving the most vulnerable behind.

power of the state. A system built on personal liberty, economic freedom, and transparent governance will unlock human potential, creating a prosperous and just society for all.

**Chapter 4**

# COMPARATIVE ANALYSIS

Case studies across countries.

### How Government-Run Welfare Breeds Dependency and Stifles Ambition

Public healthcare, education, and welfare policies differ globally, but a clear pattern emerges when state control becomes too extensive: citizens become increasingly dependent on government programs, personal responsibility declines, and economic progress stalls. This chapter compares welfare models from Europe and the United States, highlighting how over-regulation, high taxation, and unchecked state power foster dependency while stifling ambition, entrepreneurship, and productivity.

# Case Study 1: France – Bureaucracy Breeds Complacency

Overview:

France exemplifies how an expansive welfare state can erode individual ambition. With its extensive social benefits system funded by sky-high taxes, the state guarantees healthcare, education, and unemployment support. However, these "guarantees" come with heavy costs: suppressed innovation, limited job creation, and a culture of entitlement.

**Key Characteristics:**

- **Healthcare:** State-managed with long wait times and frequent service rationing.
- **Education:** Free but low-quality public education, forcing middle-class families into costly private schools.
- **Taxes:** Income tax rates up to 45%, plus employer taxes and a 20% VAT.

**Outcomes:**

**Pros:**

✓ Universal healthcare access and guaranteed welfare safety nets.

**Cons:**

✗ **Welfare Dependency:** Welfare recipients often remain on benefits for life, seeing no need to pursue employment.

✗ **Economic Paralysis:** High business taxes discourage innovation and job creation.

✗ **Entitlement Culture:** Many citizens structure their lives around maximizing welfare payments, sacrificing personal ambition for government handouts.

# Case Study 2: Germany – State Welfare With

# Market Influence

**Overview:**

Germany attempts to balance state welfare and free-market incentives. However, even its dual public-private system leads to dependency, especially among long-term welfare recipients, who face little incentive to return to the workforce due to generous state benefits.

**Key Characteristics:**

- **Healthcare:** Public-private hybrid offering coverage but funded by steep payroll taxes.
- **Education:** Free education with an emphasis on vocational training.
- **Taxes:** Up to 45% in income taxes plus mandatory social contributions.

**Outcomes:**

**Pros:**

✓ **Skilled Workforce:** Apprenticeship programs reduce youth unemployment.

✓ **Industrial Powerhouse:** A competitive economy driven by exports and innovation.

**Cons:**

✗ **Generational Welfare Dependency:** Welfare recipients remain on state aid for years, passing reliance down to the next generation.

✗ **Erosion of Work Ethic:** Those outside vocational tracks often default to government welfare rather than pursuing career advancement.

# Case Study 3: Sweden – A Welfare Paradise Or

# Socialist Trap?

**Overview:**

Sweden's high-tax, high-benefit welfare state is often praised, but reality tells a different story. Citizens face excessive taxation and have limited options outside government-managed systems. Welfare reliance is deeply entrenched, and the shrinking workforce means fewer people pay into the system while more draw from it.

**Key Characteristics:**

- **Healthcare:** Government-run healthcare plagued by long wait times and rationed care.
- **Education:** Public education funded through heavy taxes, with declining performance in global rankings.
- **Taxes:** Marginal tax rates exceed 60%, with a 25% VAT on goods and services.

**Outcomes:**

**Pros:**

✓ Social safety nets ensure no one falls into extreme poverty.

**Cons:**

✗ **Tax Dependency Cycle:** Those who succeed are punished by oppressive taxation, reducing incentives to work harder or innovate.

✗ **Welfare Addiction:** Generous unemployment benefits create a permanent underclass of welfare recipients.

✗ **Entrepreneurial Barriers:** High business taxes and regulations make starting a business nearly impossible.

## Case Study 4: The U.s. – Private Markets Vs. Government Expansion (Aca)

**Overview:**

The United States, long a model of free-market healthcare and education, took a significant shift toward government control with the Affordable Care Act (ACA). The move created more reliance on government-mandated programs, increased taxes, and reduced personal healthcare choices.

**Before the ACA (Pre-2010):**

**Key Characteristics:**

- **Healthcare:** Private-driven system with employer-based insurance and minimal government interference.
- **Education:** K-12 public schools with private options and competitive higher education.
- **Taxes:** Moderate tax rates with a top federal income tax rate of 35%.

**Outcomes:**

**Pros:**

✓ **Personal Choice:** Americans could choose their providers and plans based on their needs and budgets.

✓ **Medical Innovation Leader:** The U.S. dominated healthcare innovation globally.

**Cons:**

✗ **Insurance Gaps:** Millions were uninsured due to unaffordable premiums.

✗ **Rising Tuition Costs:** Student loans fueled skyrocketing tuition prices with no government controls.


**After the ACA (Post-2010):**

**Key Characteristics:**

- **Healthcare:** Government-mandated insurance with expanded Medicaid and tax-funded subsidies.
- **Education:** Continued student loan expansion but no checks on tuition inflation.
- **Taxes:** Increased taxes on businesses and high-income earners.

**Outcomes:**

**Pros:**

✓ **Reduced Uninsured Rate:** The number of uninsured Americans fell by about 8%.

✓ **Pre-Existing Condition Protections:** Insurers couldn't deny coverage due to health history.

**Cons:**

✗ **Premium Hikes:** Insurance premiums soared due to increased government mandates.

✗ **Reduced Freedom:** Patients faced reduced provider options and restricted care.

✗ **Economic Disincentives:** Businesses reduced full-time hiring to avoid health insurance mandates.

# Government Control Breeds Dependence

The international comparison shows that welfare systems driven by government control inevitably create a cycle of entitlement, complacency, and diminished economic ambition. When governments promise "free" services, they instead deliver an expensive system built on high taxes, suppressed productivity, and restricted personal freedoms.

**Key Policy Recommendations:**

- **Reduce Welfare Entitlements:** Limit long-term welfare eligibility to encourage workforce participation.
- **Lower Taxes & Deregulate:** Free up businesses to create jobs and boost economic growth.
- **Strengthen Private Sector Incentives:** Encourage private investment in healthcare and education through tax cuts and deregulation.
- **Promote Individual Responsibility:** Shift welfare models from entitlements to temporary aid tied to job training or employment milestones.

The path to economic vitality requires reducing government interference, rewarding hard work, and fostering a culture of independence rather than dependency. Personal responsibility and free-market principles must replace state-driven entitlements if nations wish to escape the welfare trap.

**Chapter 5**

# THE USA'S ATTEMPT TO SOCIALIZE AMERICA

## *From Government Overreach to Cultural Manipulation*

### How Centralized Policies, High Taxes, and Cultural Engineering Changed America

The United States, a nation built on the principles of limited government, individual freedom, and free-market capitalism, has increasingly drifted toward centralized control, particularly in the 21st century. What was once a country driven by personal responsibility and entrepreneurial spirit has seen a systematic expansion of federal power, resulting in economic regulation, cultural engineering, and ideological indoctrination. This shift became most evident during the Obama Administration, which used sweeping policies and bureaucratic mandates to reshape healthcare, education, and cultural narratives under the banner of "equality" and "social justice."

Initially framed as efforts to correct societal inequalities, these policies soon morphed into instruments of state control. Key sectors like healthcare, education, and media were targeted for government-driven reform, enabling a central authority to regulate not only economic behavior but also cultural values. In an unprecedented move, social narratives were curated and amplified through state-aligned media outlets and tech monopolies.

Public discourse was reshaped through policy-driven mandates, executive orders, and carefully orchestrated messaging campaigns. Media outlets and social platforms willingly partnered with the government to suppress dissent, creating a unified narrative that left little room for alternative views. As the government's reach extended beyond traditional public policy into personal beliefs and cultural norms, Americans found themselves increasingly subject to ideological enforcement disguised as progressive reforms.

What began as policy initiatives to "level the playing field" ultimately expanded into a full-scale social engineering project aimed at redefining the American way of life. The push for state-controlled services merged with identity-based activism, redefining cultural norms and promoting ideological compliance through the education system, corporate policies, and mass media. Under the guise of equity, fairness, and inclusion, the foundations of free-market competition, personal liberty, and free thought were gradually replaced by a state-centric vision of collective dependence and enforced ideology.

This growing fusion of policy-driven governance, media influence, and cultural manipulation has reshaped the landscape of American society, moving it further from its founding ideals of freedom and opportunity toward a system built on centralized control and ideological conformity. The consequences of this transformation continue to shape the nation's political, economic, and cultural reality, threatening the very principles on which the

United States was founded.

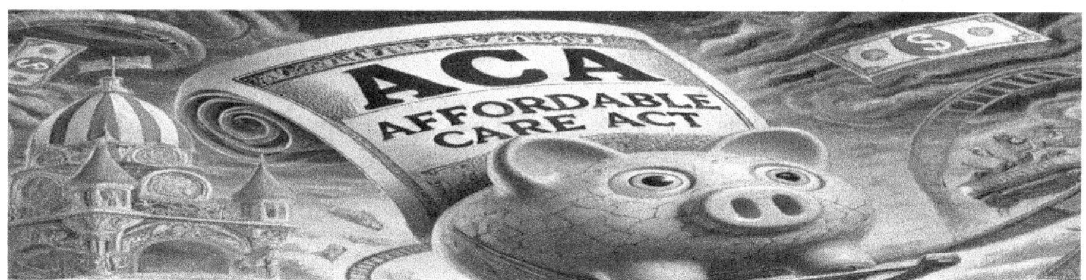

# The Healthcare Takeover

## The Affordable Care Act (ACA)

The Obama Administration's **Affordable Care Act (ACA)**, signed into law in 2010, was promoted as a transformative step toward achieving universal healthcare in the United States. It promised to lower costs, expand coverage, and increase access to quality care. However, the reality unfolded much differently. The ACA became a vehicle for expanding federal control over healthcare, reducing individual choice, and consolidating power within a few large insurance companies. What began as a policy for "healthcare reform" evolved into one of the largest government takeovers in American history.

# How The System Was Manipulated

## False Promises and Deceptive Messaging

### "If You Like Your Doctor, You Can Keep Your Doctor":

This phrase became one of the most infamous false promises of the ACA. Millions of Americans quickly learned that their existing healthcare plans were deemed "non-compliant" with ACA regulations and were canceled. The government mandated that all plans meet specific federal coverage standards, forcing many insurers to discontinue plans that didn't align with the ACA's rigid requirements.

### Cancellation Notices:

In 2013 alone, over **4.7 million Americans** received cancellation notices from their insurers because their plans didn't meet the ACA's new regulations. Instead of keeping their doctors or existing coverage, individuals were forced into ACA-approved plans, often with much higher premiums and deductibles.

## Government Mandates and Individual Penalties

### The Individual Mandate:

The ACA imposed a tax penalty on individuals who chose not to purchase health insurance, effectively eliminating personal healthcare choice. Americans were compelled to buy federally approved insurance or face financial penalties enforced by the IRS—a direct attack on economic freedom.

### Employer Mandates:

Employers with 50 or more full-time employees were required to provide health insurance or face steep fines. In response, many businesses reduced employee hours, shifted workers to part-time status, or halted hiring altogether to avoid the financial burden of mandatory coverage.

### Supreme Court Ruling:

In a controversial 2012 decision, the **Supreme Court** upheld the ACA's individual mandate as a "tax," despite the Administration's previous claims that it wasn't one. This legal maneuver legitimized what was effectively government coercion under the guise of "healthcare reform."

## Creation of Insurance Monopolies

### Reduced Competition:

The ACA was supposed to increase market competition by establishing state-run insurance exchanges. Instead, it resulted in **insurance monopolies** in several states. Many smaller insurers were unable to meet the law's costly administrative requirements and withdrew from the market, leaving a few large insurance corporations to dominate.

### Limited Provider Networks:

To comply with ACA mandates while keeping costs low, insurers drastically reduced their provider networks. This limited patients' access to doctors and hospitals, forcing them into narrower care plans with fewer treatment options.

### Rural Healthcare Crisis:

In many rural areas, only one or two insurance companies remained after the ACA's implementation, effectively creating local monopolies. Consumers in these areas faced skyrocketing premiums with no alternative providers.

## Ballooning Costs and Economic Fallout

### Premium Increases:

Contrary to promises of reduced costs, health insurance premiums rose substantially for millions of Americans. Families that qualified for ACA subsidies were shielded from the worst price hikes, but **middle-class families**—those earning too much to qualify for assistance but still struggling financially—bore the brunt of skyrocketing premiums and deductibles.

### Healthcare Costs Still Rising:

Between 2010 and 2020, **healthcare costs doubled** for the average American family. While politicians celebrated reduced uninsured rates, they ignored the reality that many families were paying more than ever for less comprehensive coverage.

**Economic Impact on Small Businesses:**
The financial burden on small businesses was devastating. Employers faced the impossible choice of either complying with costly insurance mandates or cutting jobs and reducing wages. For many, survival meant restructuring businesses, scaling down operations, or ceasing to offer healthcare benefits entirely.

# The Aftermath - A Weakened Healthcare System

The ACA's unintended consequences created a fractured healthcare system burdened by government overreach, runaway costs, and reduced patient choice. While millions of previously uninsured Americans gained access to Medicaid or ACA-subsidized plans, many more found themselves trapped in an increasingly dysfunctional system. Healthcare decisions once made between patients and doctors were now governed by federal regulations and bureaucratic mandates.

# Political Motives Behind The Aca

The ACA was not simply a healthcare policy—it was a calculated political move designed to expand government power and create long-term dependency on federally controlled services. The Administration framed the ACA as a humanitarian effort, but its design embedded powerful mechanisms that increased Washington's influence over both the healthcare system and American lives.

### Expanding the Welfare State:
By enrolling millions of Americans in government-subsidized health plans, the ACA created a permanent constituency reliant on federal assistance. This dependency translated into a powerful voting bloc with vested interests in maintaining and expanding the welfare state.

### Political Payoffs:
Major insurance providers and pharmaceutical companies supported the ACA after securing favorable provisions, effectively turning private corporations into extensions of the federal government. This alliance between state power and corporate profit further entrenched the monopolistic healthcare system.

## Promises Broken, Freedoms Lost

The ACA stands as a stark example of how government overreach, wrapped in the language of compassion and fairness, can strip individuals of choice and economic freedom. The law's implementation revealed that its architects prioritized expanding state control over fulfilling promises of affordability and access. Millions of Americans now face a healthcare system that is more expensive, more restrictive, and less responsive to individual needs than ever before.

What was marketed as a step toward "healthcare for all" ultimately became a tool for government intervention, economic coercion, and political control—transforming one of the world's most innovative healthcare systems into a bureaucratic nightmare. True healthcare reform will only be possible when individuals—not the state—regain control over their health, finances, and personal freedoms.

# Media Manipulation And Narrative Control

During the Obama administration, media influence reached unprecedented levels through coordinated efforts between the government, mainstream media, and emerging tech platforms. This alignment ensured that state-approved narratives dominated public discourse while alternative perspectives were discredited or suppressed. The concept of a free press was gradually reshaped into a mechanism for political messaging and social engineering.

# Media Control Tactics

## Mainstream Media Compliance

- **Network Alignment:** Major networks like CNN, MSNBC, and influential newspapers such as *The New York Times* and *The Washington Post* closely aligned their reporting with government narratives.
- **Echo Chamber Effect:** These outlets frequently echoed official talking points, often framing policy decisions as unquestionable and suppressing dissenting expert opinions.
- **Selective Coverage:** Investigative reporting critical of government actions was minimized or avoided altogether, while stories supporting administration policies received extensive coverage.

# Social Media Censorship

**Platform Control:** As social media platforms like Facebook, Twitter, and YouTube became the primary sources of information for millions, government agencies worked behind the scenes to influence content moderation policies.

**Labeling and Suppression:** Content labeled as "misinformation" or "false news" was routinely de-platformed or algorithmically suppressed—often without clear definitions or transparency.

**Covert Partnerships:** Revelations of government partnerships with tech companies exposed coordinated campaigns to remove posts critical of administration policies, including healthcare reforms and foreign policy decisions.

# Weaponized Propaganda

**Narrative Shaping:** Media personalities supportive of government policies were elevated to high-profile positions, framing partisan perspectives as objective truth.

**Discrediting Opposition:** Independent journalists and whistleblowers were discredited as "conspiracy theorists" or accused of spreading "fake news," silencing legitimate critiques of state actions.

**Influence Operations:** Leaks and "anonymous sources" strategically fed favorable stories to the press, often shaping public opinion before facts could be independently verified.

# Impact On Free Press And Public Trust

This coordinated media environment blurred the lines between journalism and political advocacy, undermining the press's role as a watchdog of democracy. Key consequences include:

**Public Mistrust:** Trust in media institutions plummeted as news consumers recognized the heavy bias in reporting and a lack of transparency in content moderation practices.

**Polarized Society:** The suppression of alternative views deepened political polarization, leaving the public increasingly divided along ideological lines.

**Erosion of Free Speech:** Censorship efforts normalized the restriction of free speech under the guise of combating "misinformation," setting a dangerous precedent for future administrations.

## A Call For Media Accountability

Restoring media integrity requires transparency in content moderation practices, protection of whistleblowers, and accountability for news organizations complicit in spreading politically motivated narratives. The public's right to access unbiased, fact-driven journalism must be defended to preserve a functioning democracy and a truly free press.

## Social Engineering Through Education

The U.S. education system has evolved from a platform for academic development into a tool for advancing government-approved ideologies. The shift toward ***Critical Race Theory (CRT), gender ideology, and social justice activism*** has transformed curricula in public schools and universities. Traditional values of critical thinking, academic excellence, and free intellectual debate have been displaced by identity politics and ideological conformity.

## Educational Indoctrination Tactics

## Revisionist History

**Narrative Reframing:** American history curricula increasingly emphasize themes of systemic oppression and racial inequality, often portraying the nation's founding as inherently racist and unjust.

**Historical Distortion:** Key historical events are selectively highlighted or reinterpreted through the lens of racial grievance, fostering guilt over national pride.

**Impact:** Students develop a skewed understanding of U.S. history, emphasizing collective blame rather than personal empowerment and civic responsibility.

# Gender Ideology In Schools

**Curriculum Infiltration:** LGBTQ+ ideology has permeated classroom instruction, including lessons on gender identity and sexual orientation starting at the elementary level.

**Parental Exclusion:** Some school policies encourage discussions about gender transitions without informing or seeking consent from parents.

**Identity Confusion:** Children are exposed to concepts far beyond their developmental capacity, fostering confusion rather than acceptance.

# Silencing Of Opposing Views

**Speech Codes and Cancel Culture:** Schools and universities increasingly enforce "speech codes" and "safe spaces" that punish students and faculty for expressing conservative or religious perspectives.

**Ideological Homogeneity:** Dissenting opinions on topics like immigration, abortion, or gender identity are labeled as hate speech, creating an atmosphere of intellectual censorship.

**Impact:** Fear of social ostracism or administrative discipline discourages open dialogue, stifling genuine critical thinking and ideological diversity.

# Decline In Academic Standards

**Reduced Focus on Core Subjects:** Academic benchmarks in math, science, and literacy have taken a backseat to social activism and diversity training.

**Lower Graduation Criteria:** Grade inflation and reduced testing standards ensure that students graduate despite poor academic performance.

**Global Competitiveness Decline:** The U.S. continues to rank poorly in international education assessments, falling behind countries that emphasize rigorous academic standards.

# Social And Political Impact

### Generation of Activists

Many young Americans leave the education system with a worldview shaped by identity politics and social activism rather than critical thinking, problem-solving, or job-ready skills.

Polarization deepens as ideological indoctrination replaces balanced education, creating a politically charged society prone to conflict.

## Weakened National Unity

Emphasizing group identity over shared national values fractures societal cohesion, making Americans more divided and less resilient in the face of national challenges.

## Workforce Unpreparedness

With declining math, science, and literacy skills, graduates are ill-equipped for careers in competitive global industries, weakening the U.S. economy's future prospects.

## Restoring Academic Integrity

The only path forward is a return to academic fundamentals focused on merit-based achievement, objective historical analysis, and free intellectual inquiry. Education must be depoliticized, with parental involvement restored as a cornerstone of student development. Teaching factual history, promoting open debates, and ensuring transparency in curriculum design are essential steps toward fostering a generation capable of critical thinking, innovation, and civic responsibility.

# Cultural Manipulation

*Redefining Social Norms*

During the Obama administration, cultural institutions—including entertainment, sports, and corporate brands—became platforms for advancing state-endorsed social agendas. From "woke capitalism" to identity-driven media representation, these shifts reshaped societal norms. Corporate giants, media conglomerates, and even sports leagues adopted politically correct narratives, often under pressure from government agencies, activist groups, and social media campaigns.

# Cultural Overhaul Tactics

### Corporate Compliance – The Rise of "Woke Capitalism"

### Social Justice Branding:
Major corporations like Nike, Disney, and Coca-Cola adopted politically charged messaging in their marketing campaigns, aligning with progressive causes such as racial justice, LGBTQ+ rights, and environmental activism.

### Corporate Fear of Boycotts:
Companies faced intense public and media scrutiny, with the threat of organized boycotts forcing many to adopt politically correct positions, regardless of shareholder or customer preferences.

### Token Activism:
Businesses often engaged in "virtue signaling," making symbolic donations or statements with minimal long-term commitment to the causes they claimed to support.

### Example:

Corporate-sponsored events like Pride Month celebrations and diversity workshops became industry norms, often mandating participation from employees regardless of personal beliefs.

## Entertainment Industry Propaganda

**Media Control:**
Hollywood, streaming platforms, and music labels increasingly integrated politically charged narratives into movies, TV shows, and music videos. Traditional family dynamics were frequently redefined, with alternative lifestyles promoted as mainstream while conservative values were portrayed as outdated or prejudiced.

**Scripted Social Commentary:**
Screenplays and music lyrics often contained progressive messaging, from gender identity advocacy to anti-capitalist rhetoric, shaping audience perceptions without open debate.

**Award Show Politics:**
Cultural awards such as the Oscars, Emmys, and Grammys transformed into political platforms where celebrities delivered speeches championing progressive causes, turning entertainment events into ideological broadcasts.

**Example:**

TV series like *Supergirl*, *The Handmaid's Tale*, and *13 Reasons Why* were praised for promoting social justice themes while receiving criticism for overtly political storytelling.

## Cancel Culture – Silencing Dissenting Voices

**Public Censorship:**
Celebrities, business leaders, and even private citizens who expressed views contrary to progressive narratives faced online

harassment, job loss, and public disgrace.

**Social Media Lynch Mob:**
Platforms like Twitter, Facebook, and Instagram facilitated "cancel culture" campaigns, allowing mobs to digitally attack individuals with opposing views until they were professionally and socially ruined.

**Career Destruction:**
People accused of politically incorrect speech were often blacklisted from their industries, with companies eager to distance themselves from any controversy, regardless of context or intent.

**Example:**

Comedians like Kevin Hart lost high-profile jobs over old tweets, while journalists and academics were dismissed for expressing opinions deemed politically incorrect.


## The Engine Behind The Cultural Shift

The rapid cultural transformation in the U.S. was not purely organic but carefully orchestrated by a combination of media conglomerates, corporate stakeholders, and activist-driven organizations. Institutions feared government regulation, consumer backlash, and activist-led social media campaigns, forcing compliance with approved narratives.


*Impact on Society*

### Cultural Homogenization

Popular culture became a monolithic platform for progressive ideology, leaving little room for cultural or intellectual diversity.

### Social Intimidation

Fear of being canceled discouraged individuals from expressing personal beliefs, fostering a culture of self-censorship.

**Polarization and Social Division**

By forcing cultural conformity, institutions deepened social divisions, alienating millions who felt their values were dismissed or attacked.

**Erosion of Free Speech**

The stigmatization of dissenting views eroded the foundational principle of free speech, weakening the nation's democratic ideals.

## Restoring Cultural Balance

To counteract cultural manipulation, a renewed commitment to free speech, personal responsibility, and diverse viewpoints is essential. Cultural institutions must detach from government influence and activist pressure, focusing instead on authentic storytelling, customer-driven branding, and open platforms where all perspectives can be heard without fear of cancellation or censorship. Only by embracing cultural plurality can society restore its balance and rebuild trust in its institutions.

## Weaponizing Government Institutions

Under the banner of progressivism, U.S. government institutions were repurposed as political tools, suppressing dissent, targeting political opponents, and consolidating state power. Key federal agencies—once entrusted with safeguarding the Constitution—became mechanisms for advancing partisan agendas, often at the expense of civil liberties and democratic norms.

# Tactics Of Institutional Weaponization:

### IRS Targeting of Political Opponents

### Selective Audits:

During the Obama administration, the Internal Revenue Service (IRS) deliberately targeted conservative organizations, particularly those affiliated with the Tea Party movement.

### Delayed Tax-Exempt Status:

Hundreds of conservative nonprofits experienced excessive delays or denials when applying for tax-exempt status, obstructing their ability to fundraise and influence elections.

### Harassment of Donors:

Prominent conservative donors faced increased audits and public exposure, discouraging financial support for right-leaning causes.

### Example:

In 2013, the IRS admitted to using political criteria—such as terms like "patriot" and "Tea Party"—to single out conservative groups for scrutiny, triggering public outcry and Congressional investigations.

# Fbi And Doj Political Weaponization

## Partisan Investigations:
The Federal Bureau of Investigation (FBI) and Department of Justice (DOJ) became embroiled in politically motivated investigations, often targeting political opponents while shielding political allies from scrutiny.

## Manufactured Scandals:
High-profile cases were pursued based on dubious evidence, such as the now-discredited Steele dossier, used to justify surveillance of Trump campaign officials during the 2016 election.

## Two-Tier Justice System:
Allegations of misconduct involving political elites were frequently dismissed or met with minimal consequences, reinforcing a double standard in the application of justice.

## Example:
Investigations into figures like General Michael Flynn and Carter Page revealed questionable legal practices, including unverified surveillance warrants and deceptive FBI interviews.

# Surveillance State Expansion

## Mass Data Collection:
Under the guise of national security, domestic surveillance programs expanded dramatically, enabling warrantless data collection on millions of American citizens.

**NSA Overreach:**
Revelations by whistleblower Edward Snowden exposed extensive government surveillance operations involving the National Security Agency (NSA), including the bulk collection of phone records and online communications.

**Erosion of Privacy:**
These programs operated with minimal oversight and often targeted journalists, activists, and political dissidents, undermining Americans' constitutional right to privacy.

**Example:**

Programs like PRISM, exposed in 2013, showed tech giants like Google, Facebook, and Microsoft cooperating with federal agencies to provide backdoor access to private data, sparking international outrage.

# Consequences Of Institutional Abuse

**Public Trust Erosion:**

The weaponization of federal institutions shattered public confidence in impartial governance, fostering widespread distrust of government agencies and electoral processes.

**Suppression of Dissent:**
Political opponents, activists, and journalists critical of government policies faced harassment, legal intimidation, and public defamation.

**Normalized Overreach:**
The precedent set by these abuses normalized government overreach, expanding state power and reducing individual freedoms under the guise of protecting national security and ensuring "fairness" in public discourse.

**Politicized Justice:**
The selective enforcement of laws created a politicized legal system where consequences depended on political affiliation rather than objective legal standards.

## A Call For Institutional Reform

Restoring integrity to government institutions requires comprehensive reform, including increased transparency, stronger Congressional oversight, and strict legal accountability for officials who misuse power. Judicial independence must be safeguarded, and surveillance programs must be limited to cases involving credible national security threats. Only by ensuring equal treatment under the law and reducing partisan interference can federal institutions regain public trust and function as intended—protecting constitutional freedoms, not political agendas.

## From Freedom To Control

*America's Shift Toward State-Driven Policies*

The Obama Administration's push for socialized policies marked a defining moment in America's political and cultural trajectory. What was marketed as "affordable healthcare," "equity," and "social justice" gradually evolved into a system of expanded government control, where individual freedoms were eroded under the guise of societal improvement. Government overreach extended into every facet of life—from healthcare and business regulation to media narratives and cultural norms—reshaping the country in ways that stifled free enterprise, silenced dissent, and institutionalized ideological conformity.

Economic Suppression Through Government Mandates
**Business Regulation:**
Policies like the Affordable Care Act (ACA) imposed crippling mandates on businesses, forcing employers to provide government-approved healthcare coverage or face heavy fines. Small businesses bore the brunt of these regulations, discouraging expansion, hiring, and innovation.
**High Corporate Taxes:**
The U.S. corporate tax rate, combined with extensive regulatory compliance costs, drove businesses offshore or into closure, hollowing out American industry and weakening global competitiveness.
**Welfare State Expansion:**
Social welfare programs were expanded without meaningful reforms, encouraging dependency over productivity. Safety nets designed to be temporary evolved into permanent entitlement systems, trapping generations in poverty rather than lifting them out of it.

# Media Domination And Narrative Engineering

**State-Backed Media Narratives:**
Corporate media outlets, often aligned with the administration's ideological goals, acted as extensions of government messaging. Stories critical of state policies were downplayed or dismissed as conspiracy theories, while favorable narratives were amplified relentlessly.

**Social Media Censorship:**
Social media platforms like Twitter, Facebook, and YouTube collaborated with government agencies to suppress "misinformation," frequently silencing dissenting views. Political censorship disguised as "content moderation" shifted online discourse toward progressive talking points while marginalizing opposing perspectives.

# Educational Indoctrination And Cultural Manipulation

**Curriculum Overhaul:**
Public schools and universities transformed into ideological training grounds. Critical Race Theory, gender identity activism, and environmental alarmism were embedded into curricula, reframing traditional academic subjects through a highly politicized lens.

**Social Engineering in Media and Culture:**
Entertainment industries pushed state-approved narratives through TV shows, movies, and music, redefining societal norms and shaping public opinion. Traditional values such as family cohesion, merit-based success, and personal responsibility were replaced with identity-driven messaging emphasizing group victimhood and entitlement.

**Corporate Compliance with Cultural Activism:**
Major corporations adopted "woke capitalism," pushing social justice narratives in advertising, hiring practices, and product messaging. Businesses not complying faced public backlash, boycotts, and even government investigations.

# Expansion Of State Surveillance And Legal Overreach

**Mass Surveillance:**
Under the guise of "national security," mass surveillance programs like PRISM and the NSA's data collection efforts targeted millions of Americans, violating constitutional protections against warrantless searches.

**Weaponization of Federal Agencies:**
Institutions such as the IRS, DOJ, and FBI became politically weaponized, targeting conservative groups, religious organizations, and independent journalists critical of government policy. Legal investigations and audits were used as tools of political suppression, bypassing due process and eroding public trust in impartial justice.

# The Result - A Nation Redefined By State Control

The consequences of these policies have reshaped the very identity of the United States:

**Political and Cultural Polarization:**
Identity politics have fractured society into competing interest groups, each vying for government favoritism.
Civil discourse has deteriorated, replaced by outrage-driven narratives and social division.

**Economic Stagnation and Dependency:**
A shrinking middle class, stagnating wages, and increased reliance on government welfare programs have made upward mobility a distant dream for many Americans.
Economic freedom has been undermined by an ever-growing bureaucratic state demanding compliance and submission.

**Erosion of Constitutional Rights:**
Freedom of speech, religion, and association has come under

attack, with dissent labeled as hate speech, extremism, or misinformation.

The First and Fourth Amendments have been repeatedly challenged by surveillance programs, censorship initiatives, and speech codes.

## Restoring Freedom - A Return To Foundational Values

To reclaim individual freedom, the U.S. must return to the principles that built the nation:

**Limited Government:** Reducing bureaucratic overreach, deregulating the economy, and decentralizing power from Washington, D.C.

**Personal Responsibility:** Encouraging self-reliance, entrepreneurship, and innovation through economic policies that reward hard work rather than subsidizing dependency.

**A Free Press and Open Dialogue:** Protecting free speech, supporting independent journalism, and holding media companies accountable for bias and censorship.

**Accountable Institutions:** Reforming federal agencies to ensure they operate within constitutional limits and respect the rule of law.

## The Crossroads Ahead

Without decisive action, the U.S. risks following the same path as failed socialist experiments throughout history—where promises of equality give way to authoritarian control, economic collapse, and societal decay. The future depends on rejecting government overreach, embracing individual liberty, and fostering a culture that values merit, responsibility, and freedom of thought. Only by restoring these core values can America reclaim its place as a beacon of liberty and opportunity for future generations.

# CONCLUSION

*Privatized Healthcare and Education Outperform Socialized Services*

The historical development of public healthcare and education reflects a paradox of noble intentions undermined by systemic flaws. While designed to ensure equal access and reduce societal disparities, these systems often fall victim to inefficiency, political manipulation, and economic mismanagement.

Public services operate within sprawling bureaucratic structures that prioritize administrative compliance over service delivery. Redundant oversight, slow decision-making, and rigid protocols result in long wait times for healthcare and declining educational standards. Political agendas often dictate policies instead of actual public needs. Contracts are frequently awarded based on political loyalty rather than merit, diverting essential funds to politically connected entities. In education, curricula are influenced by ideological narratives instead of focusing on academic excellence.

High taxation sustains these services, reducing disposable income and limiting economic mobility. Small businesses and entrepreneurs are stifled by heavy tax burdens, regulatory mandates, and mandatory social contributions. While access to services is theoretically universal, quality often suffers due to underfunding, staff shortages, and outdated infrastructure. Overburdened public hospitals and underperforming schools frequently deliver substandard outcomes compared to their private counterparts.

Welfare-driven models incentivize reliance on state services rather than fostering self-sufficiency. Multi-generational dependency becomes a societal norm, perpetuating poverty cycles instead of breaking them through education and skill development.

In contrast, privatized systems driven by competition and consumer choice provide significant advantages. Private enterprises must deliver high-quality services or risk losing customers, fostering innovation and continuous improvement. Competition leads to cutting-edge technology adoption in healthcare and modern teaching methods in education. Private organizations face direct consequences for poor performance, while public systems are often shielded by government protections. Profit-driven models ensure efficient resource allocation and minimize waste.

Consumers can choose providers that align with their preferences, whether selecting specialized medical care or choosing educational programs suited to their children's needs. Customization fosters a more personalized approach to service delivery. A thriving private sector stimulates economic growth through job creation, investment in new technologies, and expanded service offerings. Tax revenue from a growing economy can be reinvested into public infrastructure without imposing higher individual tax burdens.

While public healthcare and education systems aim for universal equality, they often fall short due to inefficiency, corruption, and a lack of innovation. In contrast, privatized models driven by market competition and consumer choice consistently produce superior results by aligning service quality with economic incentives. To balance equity and efficiency, countries must explore mixed models that retain public safety nets while fostering competition and accountability within essential services.

# Why Privatized Services Excel

Privatized services consistently outperform government-run systems due to inherent *advantages in efficiency, quality, accountability, and economic growth*. Unlike public institutions bound by bureaucracy and political agendas, private providers operate in a competitive environment where customer satisfaction drives success.

# Economic Efficiency

Market-driven systems encourage innovation by forcing private providers to adopt new technologies, streamline operations, and improve services to remain competitive. Unlike state-run programs, where funding often flows regardless of performance, private enterprises allocate resources based on supply, demand, and customer needs. This dynamic ensures that funds are directed toward productive services rather than being lost to inefficiency or mismanagement.

# Quality Of Service

Private providers excel in both healthcare and education by focusing on customer satisfaction and results-driven performance. In healthcare, private hospitals and clinics offer faster, more personalized care with access to cutting-edge treatments. Wait times are shorter because efficiency and patient outcomes directly impact revenue. Similarly, private schools maintain high academic standards by adopting modern teaching methods, integrating technology, and adjusting to market demands for better educational outcomes.

## Accountability And Transparency

Privatized systems thrive on accountability because poor performance can result in lost business or closure. Private providers must meet clear performance targets, and transparency is a competitive advantage in securing customer trust. In contrast, public institutions are often insulated from failure due to government protections, bureaucratic inertia, and union-backed job security. Waste and corruption are minimized because financial mismanagement risks reputational damage and financial losses.

## Economic Growth And Entrepreneurship

A thriving private sector fosters job creation, technological innovation, and expanded economic opportunities. As businesses grow and prosper, they generate tax revenue that can be reinvested into essential infrastructure and public projects without raising individual tax burdens. Additionally, lower government spending on inefficient public services allows for reduced tax rates, encouraging further investment, business expansion, and higher disposable income.

## Key Advantages Of Privatized Systems

**1. Competition Drives Excellence:**
Private enterprises must consistently deliver high-quality services or risk losing customers. This creates a continuous cycle of improvement and innovation, driving advancements in healthcare, education, and other service-based industries.

**2. Accountability and Transparency:**

Private organizations face immediate consequences for underperformance, ensuring that quality, transparency, and customer satisfaction remain top priorities. In public systems, failure is often shielded by political protections and bureaucratic complexity.

**3. Individual Choice and Customization:**
Privatized services offer consumers the freedom to choose providers that meet their specific needs, whether for specialized medical care or personalized education. This customization fosters a more responsive and customer-centric service environment.

**4. Economic Growth and Job Creation:**
Privatization stimulates economic growth by promoting entrepreneurship, job creation, and technological investment. With reduced reliance on taxpayer-funded services, the private sector expands, creating opportunities and reducing the overall tax burden.

*The success of privatized services comes from their ability to align business success with public benefit.* In competitive markets, quality, efficiency, and innovation are not just goals but necessities. To create lasting prosperity and ensure accessible, high-quality services, a balance must be struck between essential public services and private-sector-driven innovation. This approach fosters a sustainable model where government supports the truly needy while allowing free-market competition to drive continuous improvement and economic progress.

# The Downside Of Socialized Systems

Socialized systems, while promising equal access and societal upliftment, often produce the opposite effect due to inherent economic, political, and operational flaws. Government control over essential services like healthcare and education fosters inefficiency, encourages dependency, and stifles economic progress, ultimately weakening the very fabric of society.

## Economic Stagnation

High taxes necessary to fund social programs discourage entrepreneurship, business investment, and innovation. Aspiring business owners face a maze of government regulations, reducing the incentives to create, expand, or hire. Government-run industries often fall victim to bloated bureaucracies, mismanagement, and inefficient service delivery, limiting economic mobility and national prosperity.

## Social Dependency

Welfare systems designed as safety nets frequently evolve into long-term support structures, fostering dependency rather than empowerment. Job-seeking and entrepreneurial efforts decline when social benefits offer a more stable income than entry-level employment. Entire generations grow up reliant on state assistance, reducing workforce participation and overall productivity. The lack of economic incentives to escape welfare deepens poverty cycles, making upward mobility difficult.

## Political Corruption And Special Interests

Government-managed services are particularly susceptible to political manipulation. Public contracts are frequently awarded based on lobbying power, not merit. Pharmaceutical companies, teachers' unions, and other powerful interest groups influence policy-making for their own gain, often at the expense of the public. Educational curricula are altered to reflect political agendas rather than focusing on critical thinking and academic excellence. In healthcare, budget allocations are often skewed toward politically expedient programs, leaving core services underfunded.

## Quality Decline

Socialized systems often struggle with declining service quality. Public hospitals are plagued by long wait times, outdated infrastructure, and limited specialist access. Teachers and healthcare workers face minimal performance incentives due to job security guaranteed by unions and bureaucratic protections. In education, overburdened schools and underfunded classrooms diminish student outcomes, further widening the gap between public and private institutions.

## Core Failures Of Public Systems

Public services routinely operate within sprawling bureaucratic frameworks that prioritize administrative compliance over service delivery. Redundant oversight, slow decision-making, and rigid protocols result in long wait times in healthcare and declining academic standards in public education.

Political agendas shape policies more than actual public needs. Contracts are awarded based on political loyalty rather than qualifications, diverting funds from essential services to politically connected entities. In education, ideological narratives replace academic merit in shaping curricula, leaving students underprepared for real-world challenges.

High taxation required to sustain public services reduces disposable income, stifling economic growth. Small businesses and entrepreneurs bear the brunt of heavy tax burdens, regulatory mandates, and mandatory social contributions, limiting their ability to invest, expand, and hire.

While access to public services is theoretically universal, quality often suffers due to underfunding, staff shortages, and outdated infrastructure. Overburdened public hospitals and underperforming schools consistently deliver subpar outcomes compared to their private-sector counterparts.

Welfare-driven models create a culture of dependency, discouraging self-sufficiency. Multi-generational reliance on state services becomes a societal norm, perpetuating poverty cycles and limiting opportunities for economic and social mobility. Without meaningful reform, socialized systems risk collapsing under the weight of their own inefficiencies.

**Key Insight**
Socialized services, though intended to promote equality and accessibility, frequently result in economic stagnation, political corruption, and declining service quality. A system based on government control fosters dependency, suppresses innovation, and limits individual freedom. Only through market-driven reforms, transparent governance, and personal accountability can societies hope to break free from the systemic failures that characterize public healthcare, education, and welfare programs.

# A Sustainable Path Forward

Based on extensive research and personal insights, the following strategies offer a balanced approach to improving public services while fostering economic growth and individual freedom. These suggestions aim to reduce government overreach while preserving essential safety nets through market-driven reforms and accountability.

# Privatization With Regulation

Introducing privatization with thoughtful government regulation can maintain service quality while ensuring accessibility for vulnerable populations. Essential services such as healthcare and education should be market-driven but guided by transparent standards to prevent monopolies and exploitation. This allows private providers to innovate while still meeting public service obligations.

## Public-Private Partnerships (Ppps)

Governments can collaborate with private companies to reduce costs, improve efficiency, and ensure high-quality service delivery. Public-private partnerships can address large-scale infrastructure projects, hospital management, and even public school improvements by leveraging private-sector expertise while maintaining public accountability.

## Competitive Educational Models

Education reform should focus on creating a competitive environment through school vouchers, charter schools, and education tax credits. Allowing parents to choose their children's schools forces public institutions to compete, driving innovation and better academic outcomes. Expanding options through homeschooling support and online learning platforms can also increase access to quality education.

## Deregulation And Tax Reform

Lowering tax burdens encourages entrepreneurship, business expansion, and job creation. By simplifying tax codes and reducing unnecessary regulatory constraints, small businesses can thrive, generating economic growth and strengthening the tax base. This expanded economic activity can support public infrastructure investment while keeping government dependency minimal.

## Why This Approach Works

Combining free-market principles with targeted public oversight strikes the right balance between economic growth and social responsibility. Privatization fosters competition, innovation, and cost-efficiency, while public oversight ensures fairness and access. Public-private partnerships create shared incentives for success, while deregulation and tax reform create an environment where businesses can grow, invest, and generate sustainable job opportunities.

By implementing these strategies, societies can break free from stagnation caused by bloated bureaucracies and excessive government control, ensuring long-term prosperity rooted in personal responsibility, economic freedom, and accountability.


**Final Thought**


**The evidence is undeniable -** privatized healthcare and education systems consistently surpass government-controlled models in terms of quality, efficiency, and innovation. While the state has a role in ensuring basic safety nets for the most vulnerable, an overreliance on government-run services fosters dependency, stifles innovation, and fuels economic stagnation.

Societies flourish when individuals are empowered with freedom of choice, businesses operate in a competitive environment, and government intervention is limited to ensuring fair competition and protecting fundamental rights. Market-driven solutions encourage continuous improvement, reward innovation, and drive economic growth—all while delivering better services to the public.

After living and working in both the USA and Europe, I have experienced the stark contrasts between two fundamentally different socio-economic systems. In Europe, where I lived from 1992 to 2012, social constraints imposed by government policies made upward mobility a daunting challenge. Most of my European friends who managed to succeed did so not because of the system, but by finding and exploiting loopholes within it. For the average person, ambition alone often wasn't enough — the state's heavy-handed regulations, high taxes, and restrictive labor laws created barriers that few could overcome.

When I returned to the United States in 2012, I was shocked by how different the landscape was. Despite the economic downturn of the Great Recession just a few years earlier, most of my American friends and family were self-employed and thriving. The U.S. remained a land where discipline, dedication, and an entrepreneurial mindset could translate into real success. The opportunities were vast, and government intervention, though present, was limited enough to allow ambition and hard work to pay off. The free-market economy encouraged risk-taking, innovation, and the pursuit of personal goals.

However, one change deeply concerned me: the growing influence of media-driven narratives promoting government dependence. I noticed how many in the younger generation had become convinced that more government involvement would improve their lives. Media outlets and educational institutions pushed the idea that state intervention could solve every problem — from healthcare and education to employment and equality. The promises of "social justice" and "equity" replaced messages of personal responsibility, individual effort, and free enterprise.

The harsh reality is that government control often comes at the expense of freedom, ambition, and prosperity. I saw firsthand how excessive government regulation in Europe crushed entrepreneurial spirit and created a culture of dependency. Returning to the U.S., I feared that the same fate could await a nation founded on the principles of liberty, individual responsibility, and limited government.

The key lesson I've learned is this: **True opportunity comes from personal freedom, not government control.** A society thrives when individuals are empowered to shape their own destinies through hard work, innovation, and self-reliance. This isn't just a political belief—it's a reality I've lived on two continents. The path to prosperity lies not in waiting for the government to create success but in embracing the limitless potential of individual ambition.

# REFERENCES AND SOURCES

## References And Sources


Books and Economic Literature

1. *The Wealth of Nations* by Adam Smith – Foundational text on free-market economics and capitalism.
2. *Basic Economics: A Common Sense Guide to the Economy* by Thomas Sowell – Insightful analysis of economic principles, market dynamics, and government policies.
3. *The Road to Serfdom* by F.A. Hayek – Examination of government overreach and central economic planning's dangers.
4. *Capitalism and Freedom* by Milton Friedman – Exploration of the relationship between economic and political freedom.
5. *The Mystery of Capital: Why Capitalism Triumphs in the West and Fails Everywhere Else* by Hernando de Soto – Insight into the importance of property rights and entrepreneurship.

## Research And Policy Reports

1.      Heritage Foundation – Reports on economic freedom and policy effectiveness.
2.     Cato Institute – Analysis of government policies, economic regulations, and market-based solutions.
3.      Brookings Institution – Studies on education policy and healthcare reforms.

## Historical Case Studies And Government Data

1.      OECD Economic Outlook Reports – Comparative economic performance across developed nations.
2.      U.S. Bureau of Economic Analysis (BEA) – Data on U.S. economic performance, GDP, and industry productivity.
3.      European Commission Reports – Insights on taxation, regulation, and welfare models in the EU.

## Media And Independent Publications

1.     The Wall Street Journal – Coverage of business, economics, and government policies.
2.      The Economist – Analysis of global economic trends and market dynamics.
3.    Financial Times – In-depth reporting on market conditions, corporate strategies, and government reforms.

## Policy Research Papers And Academic Journals

1. Journal of Economic Perspectives – Articles on economic policy analysis and institutional performance.
2. Public Choice Journal – Studies on government behavior, political economy, and regulation.
3. American Economic Review – Research on market outcomes, policy interventions, and economic growth.

## Government And Policy Websites

1. U.S. Census Bureau – Economic and population data.
2. Centers for Medicare & Medicaid Services (CMS) – Data on U.S. healthcare policies and spending.
3. World Bank Development Indicators – Global development and economic performance statistics.

# Personal Observations And Real-World Case Studies

1.     First-hand accounts of entrepreneurship and business operation challenges in France and the U.S.
2.     Observations of healthcare inefficiencies and public service decline in socialized systems.
3.     Direct experiences with education systems affected by government intervention and regulatory constraints.

These references provided valuable insights, empirical data, and real-world examples essential to crafting a comprehensive analysis of public and private service models. The combined perspectives of historical, academic, and personal experiences helped shape this book's balanced examination of government policies, free-market principles, and societal progress.

# ACKNOWLEDGMENTS

This work reflects personal experiences, insights, and observations gained through years of living, working, and interacting with individuals across Europe and the United States. The thoughts expressed are shaped by real-world encounters with entrepreneurs, professionals, and everyday citizens navigating complex health-care, education, and economic systems.

I am deeply thankful for the conversations, shared stories, and firsthand experiences that helped inform the narratives explored in this book. These interactions have provided invaluable perspectives on how policies impact lives in tangible, often unforeseen ways.

Special thanks to friends, colleagues, and mentors who shared their struggles, triumphs, and unfiltered truths about navigating state-run systems, surviving in heavily taxed economies, and pursuing entrepreneurial dreams despite overwhelming odds. Your stories bring depth and authenticity to this work.

Lastly, I acknowledge those who dare to challenge conventional wisdom, question political narratives, and advocate for freedom, accountability, and individual responsibility in today's complex social and economic world. Your determination inspires meaningful discussions about reform and progress.

**Further Reading**

For readers interested in exploring some of the broader themes discussed in this book, the following works provide valuable perspectives on economics, policy, and personal freedom:

- *Capitalism and Freedom* by Milton Friedman

- *The Road to Serfdom* by F.A. Hayek
-  *Basic Economics: A Common Sense Guide to the Economy* by Thomas Sowell
- *The Wealth of Nations* by Adam Smith
- *The Mystery of Capital* by Hernando de Soto

These works offer deeper insights into economic principles, political structures, and the delicate balance between state intervention and personal freedom. While this book draws from lived experience, these recommended readings provide broader theoretical and historical contexts for those curious to learn more.

Personal experience is one of the most authentic lenses through which to examine societal systems. This work aims to shed light on the realities behind well-intentioned policies and their unintended consequences. By exploring these stories and reflections, I hope readers gain a deeper understanding of how policy decisions shape lives—not just on paper, but in everyday struggles, successes, and resilience.

www.ingramcontent.com/pod-product-compliance
Lightning Source LLC
Chambersburg PA
CBHW061642250726
48659CB00004B/1351